THE
MOTHERLY AND AUSPICIOUS

Maurice Collis

THE
MOTHERLY AND AUSPICIOUS

*being the life of
the Empress Dowager Tzu Hsi
in the form of a drama
with an introduction
and notes*

FABER AND FABER LIMITED
24 Russell Square
London

To
my old friend
BERNARD SWITHINBANK

First published in Mcmxliii
by Faber and Faber Limited
24 Russell Square, London, W.C.1
Printed in Great Britain by
the Shenval Press, Hertford
All rights reserved
A dramatic composition by Maurice Collis
Copyright Mcmxliii

CONTENTS

ILLUSTRATIONS

These portraits, from photographs and other contemporary records, are by the artist whose pen name is
CLOUDS AND SMOKE

INTRODUCTION

The Empress-Dowager of the Great Pure Realm, whose style was Tzu Hsi, which means Motherly and Auspicious, was born in 1835 and died in 1908. The year 1861, when she was twenty-six years of age, saw her already the most powerful individual in China. For the next forty-seven years she ruled the empire, her authority steadily increasing throughout the period. How she contrived to seize power, and having got it how she managed to keep it for so long, is a story more astonishing than any related of her sex.

What manner of woman was this Tzu Hsi? In a general view we may think of her as the grand adventuress. Daughter of an obscure Manchu official, she is selected in 1853 along with other girls for service in the Inner Palace and within a year has become the Emperor Hsien Feng's favourite. Favourites of autocratic rulers have generally been content to dispense patronage, interfere with policy and regulate the succession. Tzu Hsi was an adventuress more considerable than that. As the beloved concubine of Hsien Feng she was in a position in 1854 to dominate the Court. But this did not content her. She knew that the reign of favourites is short. Moreover, she was conscious of abilities more brilliant than those possessed by the generality of favourites. Not only could she manage men by charm and guile, but overcome them by her resolution and practical resource. From the beginning she cast her eyes upward. She would rule, not through the Dragon, but from the Dragon Seat.

Throughout her life her plans were always laid with a consummate realism. She understood the bounds of the possible; she appreciated the importance of giving legal colour and an air of propriety to all her transactions; and since she gambled for the highest stakes, she had no reservations, no deed being too stark, were it necessary for success. Nor did she dissipate her energies in acts irrelevant to the grand goal of absolute power and the enjoyment of its exercise. To that all else was subordinate: when she had asked the question—where do I stand?—she stopped. And though no one had a better turn of improving phrase, morality only interested her as a political device.

While considering in 1853 how to pass from the position of

7

favourite to that of ruler, the course she should follow gradually took shape. First, she must provide the childless Emperor with an heir, thereby qualifying for the title of Imperial Concubine, which ranked immediately after that of Empress. As Hsien Feng was incapable of begetting an heir, she would have to procure one by some other means. Once the acknowledged mother of the Heir Apparent and with the rank of Imperial Concubine, she would be entitled on the death of the Emperor to the rank of Empress-Dowager and to the appointment of co-Regent with the Empress. This would give her in practice absolute power during the minority of her supposed son, for the Empress happened to be a nonentity. Having resolved on her road, she took it step by step. In 1856 she procured a child from a woman of the people, whom she successfully passed off as the Emperor's child by her, and was promoted as she had calculated to the rank of Imperial Concubine. In 1861 she destroyed the Emperor by poison, and as mother of the boy Emperor became Empress-Dowager, and co-Regent with the Empress. It was at this time that she took the title of Motherly and Auspicious, her age, as we have seen, being only twenty-six.

The Empress had now become the Empress-Dowager Tzu An, the Motherly and Restful. The joint regency lasted eleven years, though it was only joint in law, for Tzu Hsi was de facto sovereign. In 1872 the Emperor, whose reign title was Tung Chih, United Rule, was in his seventeenth year. Dynastic law required that the administration be handed over to him and that the regency be dissolved. But Tzu Hsi had no intention of retiring into obscurity and took a series of measures to meet the situation. After failing to marry the Emperor to a nominee of her own, through whom she planned to control him, and, in spite of the semi-imprisonment in which she detained him, being unable to keep him wholly separated from the woman whom he had made his Empress, she caused him to be murdered in 1875, when it had become clear that his wife was with child and that the two of them were determined to assert their rights. Then, through her control of the Household Troops, she was able to force the Council to elect her nephew, again a minor, to the Dragon Seat.

She was now forty years of age and began a second long Regency, with the insignificant Tzu An again as co-Regent. Six years later, in 1881, she poisoned her, Tzu An having heedlessly become the tool of conspirators. This left her sole Regent.

Her nephew, the Emperor, whose reign title was Kuang Hsu, Brilliant Succession, reached seventeen years of age in 1888. Here was the old problem over again. Tzu Hsi had to hand over to him the direction of affairs, but was as determined as ever not to retire. To ensure that the supreme control remained in her own hands, she allowed him to deal only with routine matters and, as a further precaution, married him to her brother's daughter, a girl on whom she could rely to watch him and report. He was an easier victim than Tung Chih, being of very weak character and stunted intellect.

This arrangement might have continued indefinitely, had it not been that events outside China, over which Tzu Hsi could exercise no control, now impinged upon domestic politics and greatly complicated her situation. Had China, as it had been for centuries, still been a closed country, almost entirely independent of what might happen in Europe, the murders and usurpations of Tzu Hsi, though deplorable at the time, would have done the empire little permanent harm. At her death, or after a court revolution, a competent Emperor would have restored the usages of the constitution, and Chinese history have recontinued its immemorial march. But the rule of this arch-adventuress coincided with the most critical period in foreign relations ever experienced by the Middle Kingdom during all the millenniums of its existence. From 1840 onwards the West, particularly England, had been encroaching upon East Asia with ever greater momentum. The political integrity of China was seriously threatened. In 1842 the Opium War was lost. In 1860 the English and French burnt the Summer Palace. As the century proceeded the pressure became stronger and more dangerous. If China were to be saved, a vast programme of reform and modernization must be initiated. But such ideas were alien to Tzu Hsi's mentality. Moreover, she knew that they would sweep her and her system of palace government away. She did not sense the desperate weakness of the empire's situation. She remained supremely confident of her ability to steer the state. It was this blind selfishness that made her career of such deadly import to China.

The catastrophic trend of events had become apparent to some of the more liberal minds of the country. These men, known as the Reformers, saw that China was in grievous peril of sinking into such helplessness that eventually it would be partitioned among the nations of the West, as India, Further India and Africa were being partitioned. Just as the men who had attempted a revolution in 1881 made a tool of Tzu An, so the Reformers induced the Emperor Kuang Hsu to lend them his support in 1898. At that time he was twenty-eight years of age, but his mind was that of a backward boy. At the Reformers' behest, he signed between June and September thirty-eight reform edicts and proposed to Yüan Shih-Kai, the Inspector-General of the most modern part of the forces, a coup against his aunt, the terrible Dowager. Her secret police, composed of eunuchs under the control of Li Lien-Ying, her Chief Eunuch, informed her in time of what was afoot and she arrested Kuang Hsu and confined him on an island situated on a lake within the Imperial City.

This act was the most unconstitutional in her career. She covered it as well as she could by an edict purporting to be signed by the Emperor, in which he was made to state that owing to the condition of his health and the confusion resulting from his edicts, he had decided to resign into her hands the direction of affairs. She was now sixty-three years of age. It seemed to her that she might reasonably anticipate a return to the happy days of her regencies when, with a council of sycophants, a quiescent people and a foreign problem which did not obtrude itself too disagreeably, she could enjoy what she loved best, the daily exercise of unlimited power.

But her situation had become very much more difficult. If a section of the upper class was convinced that the only way to save China was to modernize her institutions and make reasonable terms with the western powers, some of the unlettered people banded themselves together into a society known as the Righteous Harmonious Fists, and vowed to cut the danger at the root and drive the foreigners from the trading ports they had secured by war. These men had no wish for reform nor saw the necessity for modern arms, for they believed, as had countless other insurgents in the past, that by magic they could achieve all they desired.

In spite of her extraordinary acuteness in the day-to-day business of maintaining herself in power, Tzu Hsi had much in common with the ignorant Fists or Boxers. Their hatred of foreigners and innovations seemed to her the authentic voice of old China, the true voice of the millions she ruled, and when she set them upon the European legations, which, much against her inclination, she had allowed in Peking, she believed the nation was behind her and that not only would the Barbarians be expelled, but the reformers be extirpated, the clock put back and all be as it had been. But when the utter incompetence of the Boxers was disclosed and the allied European forces entered her capital in 1900, she refused to yield and, indomitable as ever, left for the frontier provinces on what, to save face, she called a tour of inspection, taking with her the Emperor in case he should negotiate a settlement in her absence.

The aim of the European governments had been for two centuries, and still was, to persuade the Court of China to grant them the trade facilities which their economic policy required. Though now in occupation of the capital they were neither strong nor united enough to set up a new government and used their advantage to force Tzu Hsi to sign a treaty giving the concessions, which they considered imperative. She bowed to the storm, returned to her palace, gave lip service to the treaty, pretended to introduce reforms, but her whole intention, as before, was to maintain herself in power. For eight more years she continued so to maintain herself. Then in November, 1908, feeling the hand of death upon her, she despatched her miserable prisoner, the Emperor, so as to deny him the satisfaction of revenging his long miseries by reversing her policy, and in a last edict sought to block her enemies, the reform party, from any possibility of interfering with the régime.

Though the above cannot be called even a sketch of Tzu Hsi's career, it may be said to include its main dramatic elements. The problem confronting the author of the present play was how to combine them into a drama of character. Surprisingly little has been published in English about Tzu Hsi and the persons who surrounded her. Such books as exist are interesting enough, but their limitations are marked. Messrs. Backhouse and Bland's *China under the Empress Dowager* appeared only two years after the revolution of 1912. Chinese accounts of what had happened inside the secret halls of the Forbidden City had not then been published. The writings of Der Ling, such as *Two Years in the Forbidden City* and *Imperial Incense*, have only a limited importance, for though she was one of Tzu Hsi's ladies-in-waiting, she served in that capacity for only a couple of years towards the end of the reign and had no knowledge of earlier events. As she was attached to the memory of her mistress and had other reasons for discretion, her picture of Tzu Hsi is not without bias. Enough escapes between the lines, however, to show what a truly terrible figure was the Dowager. For instance, Der Ling mentions, as if by the way, that the old lady was always accompanied by a squad of floggers, who threw down and beat anyone guilty of the

11

smallest fault. She also lets drop the information that had a hair-dye she had taken the responsibility of ordering for her mistress from Paris proved harmful, she would certainly have been executed. Two other English books may also be mentioned, Daniel Varé's biography and *Twilight in the Forbidden City* by Sir Reginald Johnston. The first writer fails to come to grips with his formidable heroine, and the second proves himself such a staunch henchman of the Manchu Dynasty that he will hear of nothing against its rulers.

The present author could never have constructed the drama which follows from such sources, nor would he have attempted to write of Tzu Hsi, had there not been placed at his disposal private translations of the Chinese works listed at the end of this Introduction. The most important of these is *The True Records of Chung Ling* by Yun Yui-Ting. This man is actually a character in the play, being the Grand Historiographer in Scene 3 of Act III. Two years after the deaths of Tzu Hsi and Kuang Hsu he decided to write his memoirs. 'I rolled up my sleeves and wetted my brush,' he states in his preface, 'and set down what I had seen and heard during my nineteen years' service under the late Emperor.' After stressing his impartiality he goes on: 'This manuscript is to be locked up in my bookcase and handed down to my descendants, who will keep it secret till the Dynasty comes to an end. Then let this inner history be published and the thirty-four years of Kuang Hsu see the light.'

With the establishment of the Republic Yun Yui-Ting's *Records* were printed. They are more than a chronicle of what happened at the Palace between the appointment of the infant Kuang Hsu in 1874 and his death in 1908, for, though fullest for that period, they deal also with the whole life of Tzu Hsi, about which their author had collected a quantity of information. The play draws heavily upon him from first to last. In some passages, more particularly in Act III, Scene 3, his very words have been used in the dialogue. His descriptions of the murders of the Emperor Tung Chih and of the co-Regent, Tzu-An, have been faithfully followed. The rendering he gives of these two outstanding events is supported by the testimony of Hsueh Fu-Chen whose works will be found quoted in the list at the end. It should be mentioned that Yun Yui-Ting does not absolutely assert that the Emperor Kuang Hsu was murdered by Tzu Hsi, but he cites the facts preceding his death and declares they strongly point to foul play.

If Yun Yui-Ting is the best authority, the above cited Hsueh Fu-

Chen is also invaluable. Without the details he provides, Scene 1 of Act II, where the murder of Hsien Feng and Tzu Hsi's coup are described, could not have been constructed so effectively. His biographies of Tzu Hsi's co-Regent, the Empress-Dowager Tzu An, and of the Emperor Tung Chih's wife, the A-Lu-Té of the play, are very illuminating and are the sources upon which a great part of Act II chiefly rests. The other documents listed have their use in filling gaps, corroborating details and providing sketches of a variety of people. It must be insisted that all the persons in the play are historical and that the characters given them are deduced from the original narratives. The value of these sources will now be appreciated. Not only do they supply a coherent account of Tzu Hsi herself, in which fact takes the place of rumour, and plain statement of the surmises which fill so much of the English books about her, but they disclose a whole gallery of subsidiary portraits, without which no play could be constructed or, if it were, it would be without historical interest. Had the present writer been obliged to invent the characters here portrayed, no doubt he would have been tempted to make some of them more likeable. As it is, critics may complain that too many are evil, or stupid, or weak, or treacherous. But it has to be remembered that we are dealing with the end of a dynasty and with a corrupt Court. Persons of good character rarely live in such surroundings or, if they do, survive long to tell the tale.

The reader who has persevered so far may feel that he is now fully equipped to read the play. Yet the author would advise him first to glance through the notes which follow here and the genealogies placed at the end of them. If he is not to be detained any longer, then let him return afterwards, when the notes will serve to clear up the uncertainties which the perusal of so curious and complicated a story may well leave in his mind.

* * * * *

It was stated just now that all the characters in the play are historical persons. To this there is one exception. Wen Li, the Mentor, who appears before each scene, is a creation of the author's imagination. It will be appreciated that some method of filling in the gaps between the scenes had to be employed, and Wen Li has been made to serve that purpose. But he has a wider significance. He stands for the most conservative element in the China of the period, the civil servant, the Confucian literatus, the man whose education was confined wholly to the study of the old classical books. This class, which had always been remarkable for its loyalty to the throne, its support of established principles and its dislike of new ideas, had given stability to Chinese civilization for many hundreds of years and had produced nearly all the notable men in Chinese history. But by the nineteenth century it had become largely fossilized and corrupt, fossilized because it continued to repeat old shibboleths which had lost all their vitality and most of their meaning, and corrupt because, with few exceptions, it shut its eyes to the evils of the day and thought only of its own enrichment and perpetuation. In the best periods of Chinese history the true Confucian practised what he preached and was a vigilant critic of Emperors who neglected the Way of Heaven. But when the Manchu or Ching Dynasty entered upon its decline, the Literati had, many of them, become frauds, with fine principles on their lips, a grand style at their command, but a keen eye for the main chance and a determination to uphold a system to which they owed their privileged position in society. Wen Li's summaries of events and his commentary upon them, though they may sound farcical, are taken from the life, are not exaggerated, and show how a biography of Tzu Hsi would run, had it been written by an official historian. One of the reasons why she was able to maintain herself in power so long was precisely because the Civil Service saw that she stood for a régime which guaranteed them, and against reforms and a revolution which would be the end of them.

The episode which is the subject of Scene 1 of Act I is well known, though it has been declared by some English writers to be without historical foundation. It has its place, however, in Yun Yui-Ting's *Records*, and may be taken as true for the good reason that Wu Hui-Chen, the magistrate who gave the future Tzu Hsi the money, subsequently became a colleague of Yun Yui-Ting's. It is on record also that he was appointed Viceroy of Szechuan and so was a prominent official of the day. Yun Yui-Ting was repeating probably what he had heard from his lips and what in any case was common knowledge in the Civil Service.

The dramatic interest of the scene will be obvious and the manner in which it touches in the future Empress-Dowager's character. From the beginning she was extremely subtle, like lightning in her moves, profoundly contemptuous of men, and wholly mercenary. She had a teasing jocular humour; no matter what the company, she took charge of events, for she always knew where she was going and how to get there. Her knowledge of human nature was natural and profound. Her nerve was extraordinary and is well illustrated in this scene by the way she waits for young Wu's return, when the others, almost in a panic, urge her to leave at once. She had summed up the characters of the youth and of his father, the magistrate, the one a stupid ass of a boy and the other a corrupt and calculating official. Throughout her career these were the types she liked to work through and, worthless though they were, would advance in the public service.

In Scene 2 we first meet the infamous eunuch, Li Lien-Ying, who is in every scene thereafter and becomes Tzu Hsi's familiar and her private executioner. Photographs of him are extant, the best being in Der Ling's *Old Buddha*. He was an almost inconceivably evil man. That Tzu Hsi should have continued to employ such a ruffian for nearly half a century is sufficient to indicate the sort of person she was. His admiration for her was genuine, because he knew that she was both braver and more ruthless than himself. She was his ideal and he sought to live up to her, but she was continually dazzling him by her superior iniquity. There are people in England to-day who saw him at her funeral in 1908. His sun had set: he was a broken dejected figure.

The episode in Scene 2 of the recruitment of Manchu girls for service in the Inner Palace requires a word of explanation. The inhabitants of the Purple Forbidden City or Great Within, as the imperial palace at Peking was called, consisted of the Emperor, the Empress-Dowager, the Empress, two Imperial Concubines and a hundred or so ladies of various ranks, any of whom might be married by the Emperor, when her rank and emoluments would be increased. Besides these Manchu women—Chinese were not eligible—there were no other inhabitants except the eunuchs, who acted as cooks, butlers, house-servants, messengers, hairdressers and clerks. The members of the Imperial Clan, that is, Manchu noblemen related to the Emperor and descendants of his predecessors, lived in the Imperial City, which enclosed the Forbidden City. No one might enter the Forbidden City except for an audience or for some special duty. Nor were its inmates allowed to leave it without permission, granted only for specified reasons. To enter the palace service entailed being cut off from the world as completely as if one entered a Buddhist monastery. But it meant a life of ease and comfort, with the possibility of great honours. A Manchu girl who failed to pass the entrance examination or did not compete, might, if she were lucky, marry an Imperial Clansman or a civil servant of the rank of Viceroy, but for the gambler—and Tzu Hsi was essentially a gambler—the palace service held possibilities greatly superior to ordinary marriage.

Neither this scene nor Scene 3 are warranted in their details by any documents, but the events they describe took place and all the persons brought upon the stage are likely to have had a part in them. A word is required about Lady Niu-Ku-Lu, afterwards Empress and later the Empress-Dowager, Tzu-An, who first appears in Scene 3. As may be deduced from the text, she and her elder sister, being the daughters of a Manchu lady named Mu-Yang-O, got into the palace service in 1852, in the second year of the Emperor Hsien Feng's reign and a year before the future Tzu Hsi. Their family was rich and well connected, and the then Empress-Dowager, who controlled such matters, and was on the lookout for suitable consorts for her son, Hsien Feng, decided to make the elder sister Empress and Niu-Ku-Lu Imperial Concubine. While still Empress-elect the elder died and Niu-Ku-Lu was given her place. This event, the significance of which does not immediately strike one, had for Tzu Hsi immense importance. The young Empress Niu-Ku-Lu was an extremely stupid and silly woman, totally unfitted for her high office. It was, no doubt, very irritating to see such a person made a present of the highest rank. But this was not the chief reason why Tzu Hsi was so put out when she heard the news. The elevation meant that no matter how successful she herself might be in the plans she was then hatching to captivate the Emperor, the other would always be senior to her. She was blocked forever from the rank of Empress. Civil servants the world over will understand her predicament. But, as was related earlier in this introduction, she devised a way of circumventing it. Yet for twenty years thereafter she was harnessed to the woman. That the subtlest, most vivid personality of the period should have had to sit side by side in audience for so long with its greatest nonentity is the comedy within the tremendous drama of Tzu Hsi's life.

The reader will find little that is edifying in the character of Hsien Feng, nor, for that matter, in the characters of his two successors, the Emperors Tung Chih and Kuang Hsu. Though Tung Chih had good intentions he totally underrated the power and resource of the ruthless woman whom he called his mother. All three of them were men greatly inferior to the earlier Emperors of the dynasty. Had they been other than weaklings and debauchees, it is hardly possible to suppose that a woman, however forceful, could have murdered all three of them, and herself reigned over China for forty-eight years. This is another very relevant fact when we seek the explanation of Tzu Hsi's triumph.

Here we may interpose a word about technique. That each scene opens with the entry upon the stage of one of the principal characters, who makes to the audience, or, if you prefer, in an aside, some remark of a sententious or improving character, requires explanation. The author is following the invariable custom of the Chinese theatre. He might have introduced the device more frequently, for in China it is employed whenever a new character enters, whether at the beginning or in the course of the scene. By employing it sparingly, as he has done, he has sought a middle course in the belief that this small departure from English stage technique will not be found too stiff, while it may also harmonize with those numerous passages where the matter and sentiment are so wholly Chinese as to be completely alien to English ways of thought.

There is an interval of five years between Acts I and II, and though the Mentor, Wen Li, gives what he considers quite an adequate account of the events which took place during that time, the reader unacquainted with Chinese history may like to know rather more precisely why the British and French forced the Emperor Hsien Feng to take refuge in his hunting palace at Jehol, a Manchurian town outside the Purple Barrier, as the Great Wall was called. In Act I, Scene 4 he is represented as being much worried by his relations with the British. And well he might be, for the next year (1857) marked the beginning of the second Anglo-Chinese war. In 1858 a treaty was signed, but when the Chinese government failed to implement it, the British and French armies advanced on Peking, and Lord Elgin, as a punishment for the ill-treatment accorded by the Chinese to certain prisoners of war, burnt the principal palaces in the Bright Round Garden, a park generally called the Summer Palace. It was at this point that the Emperor fled. His position was extremely precarious, for not only had western troops forced their way to his capital, but a large section of his own people, known as the Tai Ping rebels, had risen against him and seized Nanking, the second city of the Empire. In Act II, Scene I, we see him, therefore, disgraced and without credit. In addition, his debaucheries had reduced him to a physical wreck. Tzu Hsi, then known as the Imperial Concubine Yi, had long decided on his death for the reasons already given earlier in this introduction. It is easy to understand why she thought the moment of his discomfiture afforded her a suitable opportunity to strike.

There are certain points in Act II, Scene 1, which, though adequately expressed in the text of the play for stage purposes, can be further clarified for the reader by a few notes. Thus, the poison is administered to the Emperor in the form of an aphrodisiac. This bare statement helps to raise the veil which always hid the dark realities of the Court of Heaven. And it gives us a further glimpse of the subtlety of Tzu Hsi's mind.

At a certain point in this scene three new characters appear, the Imperial Princes Yee and Cheng, and the Grand Secretary, Su Shun. It is just as well here to have some notion of the working of the Chinese Government. From one point of view it strongly resembled the Government of India before the introduction of representative bodies. The Viceroy of India was head of the Civil Service, and not only was all the administration carried on by officials, but such advisory councils as existed were largely composed of them. In the same way the Emperor of China was the head of the bureaucracy. The persons in charge of the great departments of state, such as the Board of Finance or the Board of War, were officials and not ministers in the modern sense. But such heads of departments were called Ministers, and in addition to their substantive appointments as Presidents of the Boards were members of the Grand Council. In that capacity it was their duty to advise the Emperor frankly and in accordance with law and precedent, but as their official careers entirely depended on whether he liked them or not, his power was potentially very great. If he had sufficient force of character, an Emperor might give almost any orders and expect them to be carried out. But when he was not a strong man, the official hierarchy wielded much power. In the present case, Hsien Feng was not only a weak character, but also discredited by his failures. In the list of stage characters, the Princes Yee and Cheng and the Grand Secretary Su Shun are described as conspirators. This, however, is looking at them only from the point of view of Tzu Hsi, for they planned to get her out of the way. They could more properly be described as a party of officials who, perceiving that the Emperor Hsien Feng was unlikely to live much longer, wanted to obtain control of the expected regency government. The critical reader may be perplexed by the passage in this scene where they kow-tow abjectly, after the Emperor in a rage has upset the table. If they were strong enough to attempt to force him to abandon his favourite concubine and issue an edict against his will, why should they fear an ebullition of his temper? The explanation is interesting and throws light on the nature of autocratic power. No matter how weak an Emperor was, he might suddenly order the degradation of an individual official and be obeyed. The tamest Emperor might be dangerous on occasion, for you could never tell what he might not do to you personally. So for a moment Yee, Cheng and Su Shun humble themselves. But when they see Hsien Feng sit down exhausted and panting, they pluck up courage and continue to press him.

There are further points here which the reader is likely to have raised in his mind. Who were these princes, what was their importance and in what sense can they be described as officials? As princes they were members of the Imperial Clan, which consisted of all relatives of the Emperor. The more important Clansmen held high official posts in the metropolitan government, to which they were appointed without examination. There was a special court, the duty of which was to keep them in order, and there were volumes of regulations governing their behaviour and promotion. But here again we touch a reason why Tzu Hsi was able to seize power and maintain herself. On the face of it one might think that these noblemen, either closely connected by blood with the Emperor or the descendants of his ancestors, would have been more than a match for an intriguing girl, not a member of the Imperial Clan and who at the time of this scene, be it repeated, was only twenty-six years of age. If power were to be seized, surely they would seize it. Well, that is exactly what the Princes Yee and Cheng, supported by the regular official Su Shun, were trying to do. But they were no match for their opponent. While we must see the cause of her superiority in the phenomenal force of her character and the strength of her mind, we may rightly suppose that the Imperial kinsmen were an ineffective body. There is a passage in Yun Yui-Ting's *Records* which is here to the point. It refers to a date some twenty-five years later, but is applicable in part to the year 1861. 'Formerly all the Imperial Princes,' he writes, 'were obliged to attend lectures in the Royal Study Room (Shang Shu Fang), and selected members of the Hanlin academy acted as their tutors. About the middle of the Kuang Hsu reign no tutors were appointed and the Study Room was deserted.

At the age of fifteen or sixteen the Princes and Dukes of the Imperial Clan were appointed to the Imperial Guard or acted as Aides. Clad in light furs and wearing bright peacocks' tails in their hats, they were busy all day running errands between the Chien Ching and the Chin Yun Gates. When not on duty, they amused themselves by training hunting eagles or riding horses. Then one day they would suddenly be appointed to some ministerial post at Court above the heads of permanent officials and be asked to advise on affairs of State. Having forgotten anything they ever knew about law and precedent, they became the laughing-stock of the country and, indeed, of the world.'

This passage, actually written in 1911, refers to about the year 1885 when Tzu Hsi was at the height of her power. We may well imagine that it was she who encouraged the young Clansmen to neglect their studies and lead a frivolous or sporting life, for it was part of her policy to bring forward her own clan, the Ye-ho-na-la, at the expense of the Imperial clan. The first duty of the Imperial Clansmen was to support the head of their clan, the Emperor; she had murdered two Emperors and was to imprison and murder a third. Though the Imperial Clansmen were not intelligent enough to see it or, when they did, not united enough to resist, she was in reality their mortal enemy. They were the hereditary guardians of the throne. She was methodically reducing the throne to impotence. The Imperial Clan, organized by the great Nurhachi its founder, had united all the clans of Manchuria in the early years of the seventeenth century, and at their head had conquered China in 1644. Now a woman belonging to a subordinate Manchurian clan, a clan which in those early days had resisted the overlordship of Nurhachi, and was defeated and decimated before it would join his army, was turning the tables upon his descendants. Curiously enough, an old prophecy had long been current in China that this very thing would come to pass. Though the men of the Ye-ho-na-la had submitted, one day a woman of that clan, so the prophecy went, would bring the House of Nurhachi to destruction.

Though in 1861, when Tzu Hsi succeeded in preventing the Clansmen, as described in Act II, Scene 1, from controlling the Regency, they were not such complete nonentities as they afterwards became, they must have been very different from their vigorous ancestors, or she could never have overwhelmed them in the way she did. Before the century was out their influence and capacity was so small that Yun Yui-Ting could write in continuation of the excerpt quoted just now: 'Twenty years ago (i.e. in 1891) the Vice-Minister Shu Chih-Hsiang of Kai-Ting said to me: "The Imperial House is doomed!" I asked him for his reasons and he replied: "I have been at Court for nearly forty years and I know all the members of the Imperial Clan. None of them are competent to fill a superior post. I know of not one with the ability and experience to act as President of the Board of War or to fill any other ministerial appointment. That is why I believe the Imperial Heritage cannot last much longer".'

This permits us to estimate Tzu Hsi's place in history. The modern Chinese execrate her memory because she set her personal advantage before the needs of the State. Thinking only of retaining the position she had won, she would have no reform, for that would have undermined her power, and so she exposed old-fashioned weak China to the cruel humiliations inflicted upon it by the West and by Japan. There is much truth in this, but looking deeper one wonders whether, had it not been for her, there would have been a revolution and a Republic. It was she who placed weaklings on the Dragon Throne. Had she not tampered with the succession, perhaps an Emperor of ability might have been forthcoming, a man of the calibre of the earlier Ching Emperors, someone who would have gathered round him the best brains of the country, and, like the Japanese Imperial House in 1870, have steered the country safely into the new century. Had this happened, the Ching Dynasty, instead of falling four years after Tzu Hsi's death, might be in existence to-day and the Chinese still be ruled by their Manchu conquerors. By destroying the Manchu ruling family, Tzu Hsi made the way of the revolutionary party much easier.

Continuing our commentary on Act II, we may draw attention to Jung Lu's entry in Scene 2, the man on whom Tzu Hsi was to depend in the matter of the Imperial Guard. It was clearly most important that she should have at her disposal a reliable body of Household Troops. While under Li, the Chief Eunuch, she organized a secret police force of eunuch spies and bravoes, Li being her confidential executioner, so she had under Jung Lu a military force strong enough to prevent any sudden coup. These two henchmen were the main pillars of her power. As we see later in Act III, Scene 2, the Reformers believed that, if they could strike down Li and Jung, she would collapse.

In Act II, Scene 3, when she comes upon the young Emperor Tung Chih and his Empress discussing a future in which she has no part and has him executed by Li, the mise-en-scène is taken from Yun Yui-Ting's *Records*, his account of the heavy curtains, the Dowager's approach in her stockings and her orders to beat the Empress, being followed in careful detail.

Later in the scene, when the Inner Council, consisting chiefly of the Imperial Clansmen, is ushered in, we see on the stage a representation of the grovelling docility to which Tzu Hsi had reduced the hereditary supporters of the Imperial House. There is a passage here which requires a note. When she forces them to elect her nephew, Prince Chun's son, to the vacant Dragon Seat, Prince Chun breaks out into loud sobs, and Prince Kung angrily calls him a fool. This is taken from Lo Tun-Yung's *Private Records* and may not be quite clear. The explanation appears to be that Prince Chun was not at all anxious to hand his baby son over to the murderous Dowager. He knew well that she was interested in the boy chiefly because he was a minor, and that as soon as his minority ended, his life would be in great danger—a reasonable and perfectly correct anticipation. So he wept, thinking of the perils to which he was exposing his son, while Prince Kung, whose son had been withdrawn from candidature and whose nerves were on edge, relieved his feelings by abusing him. Tzu Hsi's penetrating glance summed up the little scene and immediately afterwards she sent to fetch the child, though it was midnight and snowing, in case Prince Chun should send him away or hide him. This small episode, taken freshly from the original sources, gives us for an instant the feeling of looking deep into the haunted recesses of the Purple City.

The extraordinary fascination exercised by Tzu Hsi upon her entourage is constantly referred to by Der Ling in her various books and is the subject of a passage which we shall quote from Wu Yung's memoirs, recently translated into English under the title of *The Flight of an Empress*. Wu Yung met Tzu Hsi a few days after the episode related in Act III, Scene 4, and accompanied her, the Emperor Kuang Hsu, the Chief Eunuch Li and other members of the Court, on a long tour through the North Western provinces. He was an honest man, and finally Li could stand his integrity no longer and had him dismissed to a distant provincial post. As the Dowager said goodbye to him, she wept—she could always call up tears at will—and said she would never forget his services: he had been very useful to her on a certain occasion. Wu Yung was glad enough to get away from the highly questionable palace people with whom he had been touring for several months, but after he had left them and 'the Court travelled farther away each day, it was as though my eyes were following clouds', he writes. 'I found that unconsciously I had become very much attached. If, after being long with friends we feel sorrow on suddenly parting and our hearts cannot rest, how much more is this true in parting with those above us, our rulers and our parents! Now I realized for the first time what the ancients meant by the sadness of those without rulers. It must have been written from experience and not born of the imagination of the essayist.'

But Tzu Hsi in a good temper, deliberately charming those about her with her wit or pretended affection, was a very different being from Tzu Hsi in a bad temper. As she grew older she became more overbearing and difficult. Her ladies were afraid to wake her in the morning. Her mood varied from minute to minute. You never knew how to take her. Der Ling admits that on one occasion she had her hairdresser beaten to death because some of her hair came out on the comb. In Scene 1 of Act III she is represented in such a state of mind. Her nephew, the Emperor Kuang Hsu, is now grown up. The author has depicted him in this scene as he really was, more or less half-witted. Both Der Ling and Sir Reginald Johnston have tried to make out that he was a quiet, decent, even clever young fellow, afraid of his aunt, no doubt, but otherwise a man not unworthy of his exalted station. But more impartial observers, who knew him well, have a very different tale to tell. Wu Yung, clearly a most loyal civil servant, lets out the truth in his *The Flight of an Empress*. At the time Kuang Hsu was thirty years of age. 'The Ching dynasty palace regulations, to the eyes of those on the outside, seemed very strict, but once inside, it was apparent they were not so rigorous. The eunuchs were not too respectful to the Emperor. Although with their mouths they called him "Lord of Ten Thousand Years", they treated him like a puppet that is pulled by strings. Nor did Kuang Hsu observe any ceremony with them. If he was idle and had nothing to do, he would sit down on the floor and amuse himself with them. He liked to draw pictures on paper of a big head and a long body, and of different kinds of demons and spirits. When he had finished a drawing he would tear it to pieces. Sometimes he would draw a large tortoise, write the name of Yuan Shih-kai on its back and stick it on the wall. With a small bamboo bow he would shoot at the picture, then take it down and cut it to pieces with scissors, and throw the pieces into the air like a swarm of butterflies. His hate of Yuan Shih-kai was apparently very deep. He did this almost every day as if it were a task he must perform. . . . The sound of his voice was light and thin like the hum of a mosquito. Those not in the habit of hearing him could not understand what he said, the sound was so fine.'

Scene 2 of Act III shows the good reason Kuang Hsu had for hating General Yuan. That he should have used magical means to avenge himself on the man who had betrayed him is highly characteristic of his neurotic temperament. The historian already quoted, Yun Yui-Ting, who was sorry for him and, in a way, fond of him, and mentions all his good qualities, gives certain details which will be of interest to the alienist. After stating that he stammered badly and was generally timid, Yun Yui-Ting declares that at the slightest sound of thunder he would rush like a child into somebody's arms. Wen Tung-Ho, his tutor, was most often favoured on these occasions. Kuang Hsu liked, too, to play with Wen's beard and hair, and would put his hand inside his robe and fondle his breasts, Wen being a stoutish man. This was the poor creature who occupied the Dragon Seat, from which the great K'ang Hsi and the august Ch'ien Lung had addressed the world. Such was the havoc which Tzu Hsi had wrought. The author's representation of this Emperor in the four scenes of Act III will in the circumstances not be found exaggerated.

In the first scene of that Act, as elsewhere in the play, certain liberties have been taken with time. The defeat of the Chinese fleet did not in fact occur on the day of the picnic, but some months later. But a great deal of the art of constructing a historical drama consists in the telescoping of time and the bringing into juxtaposition of relevant events.

The third scene of the act is perhaps closer to history than any other, for a great part of the dialogue is almost a verbatim transcription from the sources. Yet here, too, the element of time has had to conform to the tempo of drama and what were five meetings of the Grand Council have been represented as one.

In this scene it was possible to sketch Jung Lu's character a little farther, but the reader may require more light if he is fully to understand the machinations which were going on. In Act II, Scene 3, it is related how Jung Lu demanded as the reward for his assistance in

24

forcing the Inner Council to agree to the elevation of Kuang Hsu, the betrothal of his infant daughter to Prince Chun's second son, Kuang Hsu's younger brother. The issue of that marriage was Pu Yi (see genealogical table), who became Emperor, with the reign title of Hsuan Tung on the death of Tzu Hsi in 1908, and some years after the revolution joined the Japanese, being appointed by them Emperor of their puppet state of Manchukuo, where he now is. That Pu Yi's maternal grandfather was Jung Lu and his paternal grandmother Chrysanthemum, Tzu Hsi's sister, is a bit of information not widely known in this country, but a knowledge of which gives the play a further touch of actuality. Jung Lu was a climber. Though perhaps the most redoubtable of Tzu Hsi's henchmen, he was not above what Yuan Chang, the Minister of Sacrifices, calls in Act III, Scene 3, 'boring from both ends'. He was far too intelligent not to see that Tzu Hsi was running great risks by employing the Boxer rabble to attack the foreign Legations, and entered into negotiations with certain Viceroys in the South to secure his position in case she failed. One is obliged to congratulate him on his address in convincing her that his intrigue was really for her benefit, and to smile when we see her also hedging by sending fruit to the beleaguered Europeans. Yet this was clever enough, and was convenient afterwards, when she disowned the Boxers and pretended to conciliate the invaders from the West.

Before we close these notes there is a matter to which it is necessary to refer. The passages in the play which hint at Tzu Hsi's moral licence may cause surprise, for in her English biographies no such reflection on her character is to be found. In a note on page 459 of his *Twilight in the Forbidden City* Sir Reginald Johnston refers to what he calls 'the scandalous stories once current in Chinese and foreign circles about the Empress-Dowager's private life' and says: 'I do not believe the stories to be true'. And then he contributes the remarkable reflection: 'It seems possible that the warping of her character, so far from having had anything to do with sensual pleasures, was due in part to an inner conflict arising from sex-repression'. This view receives no support in the Chinese sources and must have caused Chinese readers a great deal of amusement. Tzu Hsi had no scruples of any kind. She was incapable of love, but she relished indulgence. She did not openly maintain gallants like Catherine of Russia, but amused herself behind the scenes with anonymous pretty gentlemen—or, for that matter, no gentlemen. From the earliest times debauch had always hovered about the Purple Forbidden City, a palace more secret than any in the world, and when Tzu Hsi became its mistress she took advantage of its facilities. That she had reformed it, turning it into a respectable drawing-room, was one of the fancies which the English and American ladies she would receive in her later days liked to believe—to her vast entertainment.

*　　*　　*　　*　　*

How then in summary do we conceive of this extraordinary being, the Motherly and Auspicious? Certainly, one thing she was not: though she knew how to rule men, she was not like a man. One feels, indeed, that, dissimilar to most eminent European women, she had no masculine traits, but was the quintessence of the feminine, and that that was the final secret of her power. The Chinese have speculated a great deal about the theory of opposites: the most ancient part of their metaphysics hinges upon it. The masculine and the feminine are two of its polarities. When the feminine is without dilution, it is described as a violent, unreasonable, intuitive force, much feared by men because it cannot be opposed by reason. It lacks light and idea and is archetypal; to men it seems misty and occult. These are some of the terms used in such Chinese speculation. They are necessarily vague, but they are suggestive. In Europe the extreme feminine is supposed to be allied with softness and surrender. But this is not the Asiatic view; if there is apparent softness, it is the softness of the morass. The feminine has its equal place in the balance of Heaven and Earth, but its domain is distinct, and when it enters that of the masculine, it turns all upside down. One difficulty in England in understanding such a person as Tzu Hsi is the absence of her like in our history. Queen Elizabeth and Queen Victoria have some resemblance to her, but they had not her overwhelming force, the force of the female when fully concentrated. She dabbled in art, she would read the classics, she spoke of good governance in splendid edicts, but had no interest in such matters in a masculine sense. She had only one interest—to see the force she represented prevail over its opposite, to know that she, a woman, was the master of men. The English burnt Joan of Arc because they were terrified of her. In the guise of a peasant maid, she had entered and dominated that most exclusive of all masculine preserves, the battlefield. To them she seemed an earth spirit who had bewitched her associates and would have destroyed her opponents, had she not fallen into their power. Tzu Hsi was a luckier or more potent fay. She bewitched the Celestial Court till its grandest figures crept about like wraiths, stammering and witless, and, though twice or thrice in mortal danger from her enemies, eluded their grasp and died triumphant in her bed.

THE DESCENDANTS OF THE EMPEROR TAO KUANG

being the Imperial House of Ta Ching from 1821 till the fall of the dynasty in 1911–12

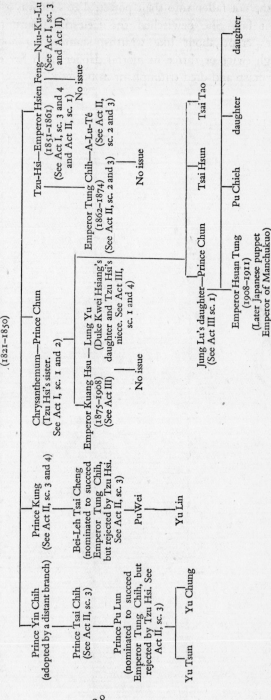

EMPEROR TAO KUANG
(1821–1850)

Prince Yin Chih
(adopted by a distant branch)

Prince Kung
(See Act II, sc. 3 and 4)

Chrysanthemum—Prince Chun
(Tzu Hsi's sister.
See Act I, sc. 1 and 2)

Tzu-Hsi—Emperor Hsien Feng—Niu-Ku-Lu
(1851–1861)
(See Act I, sc. 3 and 4
and Act II, sc. 1)

(See Act I, sc. 3
and Act II)

No issue

Prince Tsai Chih
(See Act II, sc. 3)

Bei-Leh Tsai Cheng
(nominated to succeed
Emperor Tung Chih,
but rejected by Tzu Hsi.
See Act II, sc. 3)

Emperor Kuang Hsu — Lung Yu
(1875–1908)   (Duke Kwei Hsiang's
(See Act III)   daughter and Tzu Hsi's
                    niece. See Act III,
                    sc. 1 and 4)

Emperor Tung Chih—A-Lu-Té
(1862–1874)   (See Act II,
(See Act II, sc. 2 and 3)   sc. 2 and 3)

No issue

Prince Pu Lun
(nominated to succeed
Emperor Tung Chih, but
rejected by Tzu Hsi. See
Act II, sc. 3)

Pu Wei

Yu Lin

No issue

Jung Lu's daughter—Prince Chun
(See Act III sc. 1)

Emperor Hsuan Tung
(1908–1911)
(Later Japanese puppet
Emperor of Manchukuo)

Tsai Hsun

Tsai Tao

Pu Chieh

daughter

daughter

daughter

Yu Tsun

Yu Chung

TZU HSI'S FAMILY AND DESCENDANTS

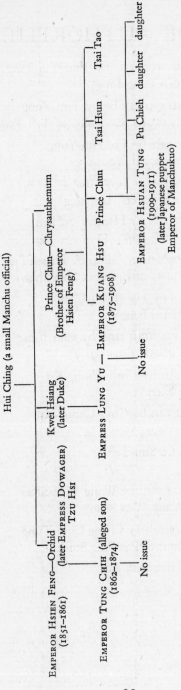

Hui Ching (a small Manchu official)

Kwei Hsiang (later Duke)

Prince Chun—Chrysanthemum (Brother of Emperor Hsien Feng)

Emperor Hsien Feng—Orchid (1851-1861) (later Empress Dowager Tzu Hsi)

Empress Lung Yu — Emperor Kuang Hsu (1875-1908)

No issue

Emperor Tung Chih (alleged son) (1862-1874)

No issue

Prince Chun

Emperor Hsuan Tung (1909-1911) (later Japanese puppet Emperor of Manchukuo)

Pu Chieh

daughter

daughter

Tsai Hsun

Tsai Tao

LIST OF AUTHORITIES

1. CHUNG LING CHUAN HSIN LU, by Yun Yui-Ting
   (The True Records of Chung Ling)

2. TEH TSUNG CHI TUNG SSU CHI by Lo Tun-Yung
   (The Private Records of the Succession of Teh Tsung)

3. KENG TSE KUO PIEN CHI by Lo Tun-Yung
   (The National Emergency in 1900)

4. CHUAN PIEN YU WEN by Lo Tun-Yung
   (Further Details of the Boxers' Uprising)

5. TZU AN TAI HOU SEN TEH by Hsueh Fu-Chen
   (The Saintly Virtue of Empress Dowager Tzu An)

6. CHIA SHUN HUAN HOU HSIEN CHIEH by Hsueh Fu-Chen
   (The Praiseworthy Purity of Empress Chia Shun)

7. HSIEN FENG CHI NIEN by Hsueh Fu-Chen
   (The Last Years of Hsien Feng)

8. SHU KENG TZE KUO PIEN CHI HOU by Chu Ming
   (Postscript to the National Emergency)

9. HAI CHUN TA SHIH CHI by Chih Chung-Ku
   (Great Events in the Navy)

10. CHIA WU CHAN SHIH CHI by Chih Chung-Ku
    (Records of the 1894 War)

11. CHIU CHI JIH CHI by Lu Shu-Teh
    (Diary of the Relief)

12. WANG WEN SHAO CHIA SHU by Wang Wen-Shao
    (Family Letters of Wang Wen Shao)

13. PAO PING TANG TI TZE CHI by Chang Chih-Tung
    (Records of the Students of Pao Ping Studio)

14. WU SHU JIH CHI by Yuan Shih-Kai
    (Diary of 1898)

A CHRONOLOGICAL LIST

OF THE MAIN EVENTS OF THE PERIOD
COVERED BY THE DRAMA

1835 Birth of the future Empress Dowager Tzu Hsi

1843 End of the first Anglo-Chinese war

1850 Tai Ping Rebellion begins

1851 Accession of the Emperor Hsien Feng

1852 Future Tzu Hsi comes to Peking

1853 She enters the Inner Palace

1854 She becomes the favourite of the Emperor Hsien Feng

1856 She produces an heir to the throne

1857 Second Anglo-Chinese war begins

1860 British burn Summer Palace. Flight to Jehol of the Emperor and court. End of war

1861 Death of Emperor Hsien Feng. Accession of Emperor Tung Chih. Tzu An and Tzu Hsi, Co-Regents

1864 Suppression of Tai Ping Rebellion

1872 Marriage of Emperor Tung Chih. End of first Regency of Tzu An and Tzu Hsi

1875 Death of Emperor Tung Chih. Accession of Emperor Kuang Hsu. Second Regency of Tzu An and Tzu Hsi

1881 Death of the Empress Dowager Tzu An. The Empress Dowager Tzu Hsi becomes sole Regent

1884 The French seize Annam, tributary state of China

1885 The British seize Burma, tributary state of China

1888 Emperor Kuang Hsu comes of age. End of Tzu Hsi's second Regency

1894 Sino-Japanese war begins on 1 August

1895 Peace Treaty with Japan

1898 Reform Edicts of Emperor Kuang Hsu. His attempt to overthrow Tzu Hsi, failure and imprisonment. Tzu Hsi becomes ruler

1900 Tzu Hsi uses Boxers to attack Legations. Allies enter Peking. Tzu Hsi and Emperor flee

1902 Their return to Peking. Settlement with Allies

1904 Russo-Japanese war

1905 China agrees to cession of rights of Russians in Manchuria to Japan

1908 Deaths of Tzu Hsi and Kuang Hsu. Accession of Hsuan Tung

1912 Fall of Dynasty

THE MOTHERLY AND AUSPICIOUS

being the Life of the Empress Dowager Tzu Hsi in the form of a Drama

CHARACTERS OF THE PLAY
IN THE ORDER OF THEIR APPEARANCE

(☆ denotes a character appearing in one scene, ☆☆ in two)

Wen Li	The Honourable Mentor
☆☆*Madame Hui Ching*	Mother of Orchid and Chrysanthemum
Orchid	Later the Imperial Concubine Yi, later the Empress-Dowager Tzu Hsi
☆☆*Chrysanthemum*	Later wife of Prince Chun and mother of Emperor Kuang Hsu
☆*Wu Tan*	Son of Magistrate of Nanking
Li Lien-Ying	Imperial Eunuch, 2nd grade, later Chief Eunuch
Niu-Ku-Lu	Imperial Concubine, later Empress, later Empress-Dowager Tzu An
Hsien Feng	Emperor of China (1851-1861)
☆☆*The Grand Physician*	
☆*Prince Yee*	⎫
☆*Prince Cheng*	⎬ Conspirators
☆*Su Shun*	⎭
Jung Lu	Vice-Captain of the Imperial Guard, later Captain, later Viceroy, later Grand Secretary
☆☆*Tung Chih*	Emperor of China (1862-1874)
☆☆*Phoenix Elegance*	Lady-in-Waiting to Tzu Hsi, later Imperial Concubine
☆☆*A-Lu-Té*	Lady-in-Waiting to Tzu An, later Empress Chia Shun, wife of Tung Chih
☆*Prince Kung*	A member of the Inner Council
☆☆*Lung Yu*	Niece of Empress Dowager Tzu Hsi, Empress, wife of Emperor Kuang Hsu
Pearl	Imperial Concubine of Emperor Kuang Hsu
Kuang Hsu	Emperor of China (1875-1908)
☆*Yuan Shih-Kai*	Inspector-General of the Forces

☆*Prince Ching*	Head of the Imperial Clan	
☆*Prince Tuan* ⎫	Members of Imperial Clan	
☆*Duke Pu Kuo* ⎭		
☆*Yuan Chang*	Minister of Sacrifices ⎫	
☆*Shu Chin-Chen*	Vice-President of the Board ⎬ The martyrs	
	of Civil Office ⎭	
☆*Li San*	President of Board of Finance ⎫	
☆*Hsui Yun-Yi*	President of Board of War ⎬ Emissaries	
☆*Lien Yuan*	Grand Secretary ⎭	

Officials, Clansmen, Eunuchs, Artists, Ladies-in-Waiting,
Messengers, Maids, etc.

An elderly man, dressed in Chinese court robes, appears before the curtain. He wears an official's hat with a coral button, which denotes that he belongs to the First Rank. The three eyes on the peacock feather sticking from it proclaim him to have enjoyed the highest Imperial favour. Round his neck is a string of court beads and he has on black satin boots with thick white soles. His jetty beard is soft and straggling, and his air so whimsical and engaging, that it sets you smiling before he begins to speak. Making a ceremonious bow, he says, as he strokes his beard:

Your humble servant, Wen Li, one-time unworthy Censor at the Court of the Celestial Empire. From the expression on your honourable faces, an expression which I am bound to say is disconcertingly barbarous, I gather you are surprised to see an Imperial Emissary. Officials of my rank admittedly seldom tour the islands beyond the pale of civilization. But there is good reason in the present case for this departure from precedent. Lately I have been resident by the Yellow Springs, a region sometimes referred to as the Great Other. What may be your honourable savage counterpart for that land I have no idea, but you probably guess to what I allude. To proceed—not long ago I was seated there under a peach-tree in my jade courtyard, engaged as usual in writing verses, and had just completed the couplet:

> Start the morning with a cup of good wine
> and the day will be a happy one.
> Start the evening by a row with your wife
> and the night will be a lonely one.

when a Palace messenger galloped up and handed me this.

[He takes a piece of almond-yellow silk from his sleeve and unrolls it. It appears to be a scroll, at the top of which in large characters the words Shen Chih—Sainted Commands—are clearly visible.]

It is a Vermilion Decree in the handwriting of Her Imperial Majesty, the great Empress-Dowager, and it reads:

'We have recently learned that a tribe of the Red Barbarians is preparing to give Our life-story in the form of a drama. Our first impulse on hearing this news was to forbid the production and to decree punishment for so arrogant a presumption. But reflecting on the ignorance of the Foreign Devils and desirous, moreover, that Our benevolence be made manifest, We resolved to extend our patronage and give them face. Now, therefore, We appoint you Imperial Commissioner and command that you proceed to the barbarian capital, where showing this Our Decree, you shall take charge of the production in Our Name. It shall be your duty to insist that only the truth is presented, that is truth respectful to Our Imperial Ancestors, and to Ourselves and Our Imperial Descendants, and sternly to repress all unseemliness and levity. Respect this. A special Edict.'

On receiving these august commands, I bade the Palace messenger farewell, drinking with him three ample cups of wine, and quoting these lines of the immortal Liu Ling:

> On the glad occasion of meeting a good friend
> A thousand cups are insufficient;
> And the bitter moment of parting from him
> Cannot be sweetened even by ten thousand.

Thereafter I immediately set out for this city.

The theatre management, on seeing the mark of the Vermilion Brush, showed a laudable compliance with the Sacred Word. I was dutifully requested to supervise the rehearsals, and whenever I found that truth was obscured, that propriety was lacking or due respect was absent, I intervened in the name of Her Imperial Majesty. Moreover, at their request, I have accepted the thankless post of Mentor, and when commentary is required I shall give it, so that even the most barbarous may understand and be edified.

Before viewing the opening scene of the great drama of Her Life, you should know that the Sacred Mother, who thirty-six years ago as Empress-Dowager discarded mortality and mounted to Heaven, was born in the fifteenth year of the Tao Kuang Emperor, or, according to your demon calendar, the year 1835. As a young girl she was called Orchid. Her family at that time [*he pauses*]—but here I am treading on delicate ground, for it has always been Her Majesty's express wish that the least said about the early days of her family the better.

Without further delay, therefore, I invite you to have a peep at her when she was just seventeen. What year that was, you will have to work out for yourselves. If you cannot do it in your head, try your fingers. And if your fingers are insufficient, I will retire so that you may take off your shoes and stockings.

[*He bows and withdraws.*]

38

ACT ONE
RISE TO POWER
SCENE I

(The second year of the reign of Hsien Feng, 1852.)

A bank of the Yang-tze River in the vicinity of Nanking, the most important provincial city in China, situated some six hundred miles south of the capital, Peking. At a distance are to be seen its gates and walls beyond the trees and villas of the suburbs. The river itself is crowded with junks, sampans and fishing craft of all kinds. In the foreground a small travelling boat is lying beside the bank. It has a cabin towards the stern, and amidships, under a piece of roofing, is a lacquered coffin. Seated on deck are three Manchu women. The eldest, Madame Hui Ching, is about forty. In her time she must have had great beauty and is extremely well preserved. Her expression is worried and somewhat helpless. She is dressed in deep mourning, that is entirely in white. An hibiscus flower, made of white cloth, is pinned into the knot of hair coiled on her head. Her lips and cheeks are without rouge. Below her cotton gown you see the ends of her trousers neatly tied with ribbons above the ankles. She wears white socks and white shoes with thick white soles. The two other women are her daughters. They, also, are dressed in white. It can be seen at once that they are both very pretty girls, but their features and expressions are quite distinct. Orchid, the elder, has a good forehead, eyes well spaced and marked cheek-bones, characteristics which the Chinese have always considered to denote intelligence, will-power and resolution, and which allied to natural beauty give a striking countenance. The other girl, Chrysanthemum, has a round and innocent face, the expression childish, uncontrolled, and rather silly, in spite of the perfection of the features. Both wear their name-flowers in their black hair, a pale yellow orchid and a white chrysanthemum. All three have the appearance of distressed gentlefolk, though Orchid's cotton dress, cut to show off her splendid figure, contrives to look quite smart.

Madame Hui Ching gets up and slowly makes a few steps forward, saying as she does so:

MADAME. My humble self, as the saying goes, is the 'still-not

39

dead' widow of the late official Hui Ching who died last winter in extremely difficult circumstances in the province of Hunan. My only son, Kwei Hsiang, is a dear clever boy. The responsibility of looking after us rests on his shoulders, and so, after selling what little we had, I sent him off to Peking to search for an official post. That was several months ago and he hasn't written. Since we could not continue living in Hunan without money, I came here to Nanking with my two cumbersome expenses, Orchid and Chrysanthemum, and my dear husband's coffin, hoping to find my old friend, Lady Mu-Yang-O. But when we called at her house this morning, we were told she had moved to Peking with her two daughters last year. Both the girls, the servants said, had got high positions in the Inner Palace. What is to be done now? The boatman has refused to take us on to Peking until we pay him the boat-hire already due. But we have no money. [*She sits down and wipes her eyes.*] What *is* to be done, children?

[*The girls come forward and sit by her.*]

CHRYS. [*nearly in tears*]. Indeed, what is to be done! But perhaps our fate is to starve here in Nanking. [*She bursts into facile sobs and moves closer to her mother.*]

ORCHID. A man's fate is in his own hands. Those who starve richly deserve to die.

CHRYS. Even if what you say is true, what can we do? We are only women.

ORCHID. Women's fate is also in men's hands . . .

CHRYS. That's what I mean. We women depend on men and . . .

ORCHID. But men's actions are controlled by women.

MADAME [*wretchedly*]. You know the boatman has threatened to turn us off. He even threatened to throw your father's coffin overboard and stop serving us food this morning. I haven't dared to look him in the face since.

CHRYS. Nor I. I was afraid he'd try and get money out of me, even.

ORCHID. That is all wrong. Why didn't you tell me before? I'll talk to the fellow.

[*She gets up angrily and her sister tries to stop her.*]

CHRYS. What are you going to do? For heaven's sake, don't offend him, when you know we cannot pay him!

ORCHID [*determinedly*]. Don't interfere with me. [*Calling sternly*]. Boatman, come here! I want to speak to you.

[*A boatman, who has been mooring the boat, looks up. He is clothed in*

40

dark blue tunic and trousers, is bare-headed and bare-footed, and has a queue which is tied round his head.]

BOATMAN [*under his breath*]. A boatman loves fresh fair wind, but he cannot live on it!

[*He goes towards Orchid.*]

What is your wish, Miss? Are you going to pay me now?

ORCHID [*looking at him severely*]. Boatman, how dare you say to Madame my mother, who is the widow of an official. . . .

BOATMAN [*sarcastically*]. A small official, a very small official who left nothing behind . . .

ORCHID [*annoyed*]. Don't interrupt me! How dare you say that you'll throw His Honour's coffin overboard and . . .

BOATMAN [*brazenly*]. I've no alternative, Miss. Unless you move it away yourselves, I'm forced to do that. I can't carry it and you to Peking for nothing.

ORCHID [*very angrily*]. Don't you know that according to law anybody who dares to lift his finger against the honourable dead is liable to be punished?

BOATMAN [*rather taken aback*]. Is that so?

ORCHID. It is so. Severely punished.

BOATMAN. I never heard that. [*recovering*] And I don't believe it. Why should you be?

ORCHID. Because the honourable dead cannot defend themselves and therefore the punishment for the offender is doubly heavy.

BOATMAN [*wavering*]. I didn't really intend to do it. I was only asking for the money due to me. I'm not to be punished for that, am I?

ORCHID. I'm not so sure. If you make a threat when asking for money, you can be punished for blackmail.

BOATMAN. I would never dare to make a threat . . .

CHRYS. But you did . . .

ORCHID [*waving her aside*]. Well, I don't say you did make a threat. I'm sure you know better than that. Now, serve us well and you'll never regret it.

BOATMAN [*reluctantly*]. Yes, Miss. [*aside*] I am sorry I ever took on this job.

[*He looks away and grumbles to himself.*]

MADAME [*relieved*]. I'm so glad that you've talked him into reason, dear. Perhaps he'll now bring us some food.

CHRYS. And I hope he'll do it soon. I'm so hungry.

41

[*Just then, Wu Tan, a young man, appears walking along the bank. He is dressed in a blue silk gown and wears a black satin skull-cap. Before reaching the boat, he stops and looks about the river. When he sees the boat, he seems to stare for a moment.*]

BOATMAN [*going up to him*]. What is it you wish to know, sir?

WU. I see there's a coffin on this boat. Is the lady, by any chance, the wife of the deceased and are those two beautiful girls her daughters?

BOATMAN [*faithful when he thinks others are interfering*]. What if they are? No loitering here! They're respectable ladies.

WU [*looking at the young ladies as if in a trance*]. But my father has sent me with 300 taels of silver for them.

BOATMAN [*immediately changed*]. Has he? Has he? Well, you have come to the right boat, sir. We have been waiting for you. Come in and deliver the money. They need it badly.

WU. Ah, my father said that they needed it badly. But he also said that I must not make a mistake. Are you sure I'm not making a mistake? Is their surname Chang, and do they come from Szechuan?

BOATMAN. Certainly. Now let me get it straight. To whom are you ordered to give the money?

WU. To a Lady Chang, from Szechuan, whose husband died recently and who has two daughters with her.

BOATMAN. Exactly right. Now, is the money a loan? And what is your name and relationship to them? I must get all these particulars clear before I take you on board.

WU. I quite understand. No, the money is in repayment of an old debt which my father owes them. My name is Tan, and my father is Wu Hui-Chen, the magistrate of Nanking. He is an old friend of theirs.

BOATMAN. I see. Now wait for me here.

[*He goes on board and addresses Madame in a whisper.*]

Ma'am, there is a nice sum of money waiting for you . . . 300 taels! All you have to do is to receive a young man whose name is Tan, and whose father, Wu Hui-Chen, is the magistrate here. He says his father is an old friend of the family. You'll agree to that, won't you? The friendship means 300 taels. Oh, and another point. You are to have come from Szechuan, instead of Hunan.

[*As he sees Madame is trying to protest, he goes on pressingly.*]

What is it whether you come from one province or from another? The sum will see you to Peking, and back if you like. Also, he said that your name is Chang. Surely you'll not quarrel with a young fool merely because of a slight difference in a name! Come, come, Ma'am, we must have money for our food! You don't expect us all to starve, do you?

MADAME. This is monstrous! I'll never allow you to do this!

CHRYS. The young man seems very nice. It's a shame to cheat him.

[*During all this time Orchid, responding to Wu's glances and smiles from a distance, is thinking hard. The Boatman looks appealingly at her. She calmly signs to him that she understands.*]

ORCHID. Bring the gentleman on board, please.

BOATMAN [*fervently*]. And you'll corroborate all I've told you, won't you, Miss Orchid?

ORCHID [*non-committally*]. Leave everything to me.

[*The Boatman ushers in young Wu, who makes his bow to Madame, but looks at Orchid all the time.*]

WU. My humble father, Wu Hui-Chen, offers his sincerest condolences to you, Lady Chang, and he . . .

MADAME. Stop, young man, I'm not . . .

[*The Boatman groans in despair.*]

ORCHID. Excuse me, but my mother is not very well, and does not like being reminded of my father's death.

CHRYS. Oh, how can you, Orchid! Aren't you ashamed to let him call her Madame Chang?

[*The Boatman looks as if he were going to tear his clothes.*]

ORCHID [*frowning at Chrysanthemum and giving Wu Tan a dazzling smile*]. You must excuse my little sister; she has only country manners and can't express herself properly. What she means is, she doesn't like hearing such an old friend of the family using so stiff a form of address. And I quite agree with her. I wish you wouldn't.

WU. I beg your pardon. For a matter of fact, I remember now, my father told me to call your mother 'dear aunt'. I'm always making mistakes like that. [*He begins searching in his clothes.*] Now where is it? I have a little envelope for you . . . if I can find it. [*Suddenly finding envelope*] Ah! here it is. I thought I'd dropped it. What would father have said if I had! It contains the money he owes you.

[*He offers the envelope. Madame turns away.*]

CHRYS [*not to be suppressed*]. But you don't owe us anything.

BOATMAN [*beseechingly*]. Don't say that, please, Miss.

43

ORCHID [*with a threatening look at Chrysanthemum and an even more dazzling smile for Wu*]. My sister is trying to make up for her bad manners just now. Of course, we had long forgotten this trifling debt. Your father ought not to have bothered about it. [*Taking envelope.*] This is, indeed, kind. We are very grateful.

WU. Please see if the money is correct.

ORCHID [*counting the notes*]. Fifty, one hundred, one fifty, two hundred, two fifty, three hundred taels. Correct!

BOATMAN [*casting up his eyes in relief and thankfulness*]. Oh, merciful Heaven!

WU. That is what he said was owing.

ORCHID. Oh, no! Not owing. We'd far rather think of it as a gift.

BOATMAN. Certainly a gift!

WU. That is very polite of you.

ORCHID. I suppose your father has been doing pretty well in recent years?

WU. Oh, yes, this post is yielding a very good profit.

ORCHID. How do you mean exactly?

WU [*naïvely*]. Well, you see, my father is an extremely shrewd business man and he foresaw that the 2,000 taels with which he bought the post of Magistrate here would be an excellent investment.

ORCHID. An investment?

WU [*who is certainly a very ingenuous young ass*]. Yes. You see, he is the best judge in the world. When he tries a case I have to weigh the bribe-silver sent in by both sides in the back of the court. If the plaintiff sends in 500 taels and the defendant 1,000, I strike the gong once and down goes the vermilion pen as he declares the case dismissed. On the other hand, if the plaintiff sends in 1,500 taels and the defendant only 1,200, I strike the gong twice, and the vermilion pen pronounces immediately for the plaintiff.

ORCHID [*smiling*]. But if the plaintiff sends in 2,000 taels and the defendant also sends in 2,000, what is to be done?

WU. Then I beat the drum, and he throws away his vermilion pen, and adjourns the court pending further evidence.

ORCHID [*very much amused*]. Ha, ha! A very good method indeed! Since your father is such a clever business man, please go back and tell him that the 300 taels he sent us will prove the best investment he ever made.

WU. An investment? What do you mean?

ORCHID [*coolly*]. You run home and tell your father that a

Manchu family heard about your inquiries and has obtained your 300 taels under false pretences.

[*Young Wu is quite dumbfounded. He tries to interrupt but Orchid signs him to be silent.*]

Now, listen to me. Tell your father that we are not of the Chang family, but of the Ye-ho-na-la clan, and furthermore, that we are not his friends, but are connected with Lady Mu-Yang-O, one of whose daughters has just become Empress-Elect. Tell him that the money is badly needed and that we shall never forget this timely loan. Tell him about my mother and my sister, and tell him we are very grateful.

WU [*enthralled by her personality*]. May I . . . May I tell him about you?

ORCHID. Of course you may. And lay the blame on me. You are entirely innocent.

WU. No! No! I don't mean that. May I tell him what an extraordinarily beautiful and clever girl you are?

ORCHID. That is very nice of you. But I shall have to be much cleverer than this if I'm to accomplish all I plan to do. Now you run along to your father and I'll wait here to see that you are let off lightly. Say the money is still untouched if he wants it back.

WU [*beginning to leave*]. I hate having to go. I don't mean having to tell my father but . . . I do want to see you again.

BOATMAN [*aside*]. You may be able to see her again, but you'll never see your money again.

WU [*turning back*]. And I don't even know your name yet! May I ask . . . ?

ORCHID. Orchid. It is only a pet name but very easy to remember.

WU [*quite overcome*]. I will never forget it. [*still lingering*] Miss Orchid, as I'm sure to be scolded by my father no matter what happens, please spend as much money as you need—no, as much as you like—and leave Nanking immediately.

ORCHID [*smiling*]. Don't worry about us. Off you go! Your father will be anxious about you by now.

[*When Wu is gone, Madame Hui Ching and Chrysanthemum look at Orchid in amazement. They are both frightened and angry.*]

MADAME. What game are you playing? I never approved of your cheating the poor young man, but now that you have his money you offer to give it back to his father! This is all beyond me.

ORCHID [*carelessly*]. You'll see, everything will be all right.

CHRYS [*almost in tears*]. But his father will come, and we may be arrested!

ORCHID. To get on in this world one has to take risks.

CHRYS. But it was unnecessary. You needn't have told the boy at the end. We must now leave at once. Quick, tell the boatman to set sail before the old man arrives.

ORCHID [*calmly*]. That is not playing the game. We must act honestly, you know.

MADAME. Where was your honesty when you took the money?

ORCHID. I meant it to be only a loan. I shall repay it . . . perhaps ten times or even a hundred times over. We had to get money now.

CHRYS [*getting up*]. Then we must pay the boatman and tell him to start at once. I don't want to go to prison!

ORCHID [*who has summed up in her own mind the character of both father and son*]. You may tell him to start, but I must wait if only for a glimpse of that young man again. He is sure to come back. He is as good as Kwei Hsiang, my brother.

MADAME [*utterly confused*]. But you've always said that my poor boy Kwei Hsiang was useless!

ORCHID. Yes! That is exactly what I mean!

[*During this conversation the Boatman has been making preparations to set sail. Orchid is watching him out of the corner of her eye. At last, when she sees he is on the point of untying the rope, she calls him to her.*]

Come here, Boatman. Do you want me to pay you?

BOATMAN. Heaven above knows how much I want that, Miss.

ORCHID. Then stop fooling about and wait for the young man to return.

BOATMAN. Let's go, I say, while we have the chance . . . [*correcting himself when he sees Orchid's frown*] I mean while the wind is fair! You don't want to be chained in a place for the rest of your life simply because you've missed the fair wind? No, I can't stop! I simply dare not stop!

[*He begins to untie the rope again.*]

ORCHID [*showing him the envelope*]. Look, Boatman, what's in here?

BOATMAN. Ah, the money!

ORCHID. If you don't leave that rope alone, I'll throw it into the river.

[*Her face is so determined that the Boatman is convinced she will carry out her threat. Quite horrified he stands up. At that moment he sees Wu Tan hastening along the bank. He points him out to Orchid.*]

46

BOATMAN. Look, Miss, here he comes. Let us be off at once! Another second and it will be too late.

ORCHID. Ah, Mr. Wu, here you are at last! We had almost given you up. But I couldn't sail without seeing you once more.

BOATMAN [excusing himself]. I was only saying we shouldn't miss the wind.

WU [out of breath]. Oh, please don't think that I want to stop you. I ran back just to tell you it was all right. My father said it might be a risky investment, but it was worth risking. But he hopes you won't forget to mention us to your friends at Court.

ORCHID. Why should I mention you to my friends at Court?

WU [dashed]. Oh!

ORCHID. But perhaps I'll be at Court myself! Listen, your father paid 2,000 taels for the post of magistrate and he thought it a good bargain. Tell him that this investment of 300 taels may make him a viceroy one day.

WU [astonished]. A viceroy!

ORCHID. Yes, a viceroy! Farewell, Mr. Wu, son of a future viceroy [turning to the Boatman]. Now, untie the rope. Away we go!

BOATMAN [with profound admiration in his voice]. Yes, your Ladyship!

[Orchid raises her hand and they all retire.]

END OF SCENE ONE

[*Wen Li enters displeased and says in an offended tone*]:

I was painfully surprised to find my instructions ignored. The Old Ancestor—I am speaking of course of the Sacred Mother—would in girlhood have shown more deference to Her parent than the Orchid whom you have just seen, for the principles of filial piety always governed Her whole conduct. However, the deviation may be condoned, as Her motive was clearly shown to be filial.

There is, moreover, this to be said, that the Sacred Mother always took a very decided line in an emergency, as you will later see, for during Her long life She emerged triumphantly from one emergency after another. It may, therefore, be that She will not altogether object to being represented in youth as a trifle forward. I certainly hope that this view is correct.

Now, you must suppose that the Lady Hui Ching and her two daughters have arrived at Peking and that relatives there have assigned them a small house. The address was Pewter Lane in the Tartar City. What has happened to that pillar of their family, Master Kwei Hsiang, I dare not inquire for the reasons I have already given. I am inclined to think that he has disappeared once more with as much of the 300 taels as he was able to wheedle out of his fond parent.

The year is the third of the reign of Hsien Feng and his mother, the Empress Dowager, in accordance with precedent, is about to select a number of Manchu girls for the Inner Palace. As Manchus, both Orchid's and Chrysanthemum's names were on the list of those eligible. Since such a recruitment occurred only during the first few years of a young Emperor's reign, how fortunate it was for China that Orchid arrived in Peking just in time for the selection.

[*He bows hurriedly and retires.*]

SCENE II

(The third year of the reign of Hsien Feng, 1853.)

The house in Pewter Lane is not impressive outside nor is it beautiful within. The furniture is shabby, what there is of it, and no pictures hang on the walls. It is evident that the occupants are far from well off. But the place has been kept tidy, and is particularly so to-day as the inmates are expecting a visit from the Imperial eunuchs, who are on their rounds making a first inspection of candidates for the Inner Palace. Madame Hui Ching, who is now dressed in rich dark blue silk, appears.

MADAME. To bring up daughters is a miserable job. As soon as you've done everything for them, sedan chairs are waiting outside your gate to take them away from you! [calling aloud] Orchid! Chrysanthemum! Let me see whether you look all right. Li Lien-Ying, the eunuch, will be here any minute and you must make him think he has never seen such beautiful girls before! Come out, children! What are you doing?

CHRYS. Coming, Mother.

[Chrysanthemum, profusely rouged and powdered, appears in a long pink dress. On her black satin head-dress she has pinned several large, rather gaudy, artificial flowers, which clash with the pink. Her earrings, hairpins and bracelets are too conspicuous and her necklace is badly made. She carries a big green handkerchief, which she sometimes tucks between the buttons under her right armpit. In spite of her beauty she has made herself look vulgar but her mother does not think so.]

MADAME [beaming]. My little Chrysanthemum, you are sure to captivate anyone who has eyes! Turn around, my dear, and let me see how you look from behind. Nice, very nice! Now, when they come in I want you to be sitting down, pretending to do your embroidery. Then just stand up, make your little bow, and sit down again and go on sewing quietly. Let mother do all the talking for you. But how I wish we had enough money to tip the eunuchs so that you needn't worry about the result! Still, with your looks and a little persuasion from your mother, you stand a very good chance, I think.

CHRYS. [sitting down and taking up embroidery]. I daresay, if necessary, I could persuade them too!

MADAME. Of course! But you must be careful to speak nicely, my dear. Orchid, are you ready? [*no answer*] What's happened to the girl?

[*Li Lien-Ying, an influential eunuch, followed by another eunuch, appears. He is young, tall, good-looking, and his glance is quick and crafty. Cool, hard, insolent, he distils a disconcerting atmosphere. The other is a mere servant, middle-aged, small, wizened, a low fawning sharp fellow. Li advances to the middle of the down stage, without more than a perfunctory acknowledgment of the ladies' low bows.*]

LI. Not much of a house, this one!

SERVANT [*at his heels*]. Hardly worth calling at, I fear, sir.

LI. Waste of time, I should think. But the forms have to be filled up.

SERVANT. The girl doesn't look too bad, though.

LI. H'm [*after a casual glance over Chrysanthemum, who is trembling at her embroidery work*]. Well, if they can afford the usual tip, I wouldn't mind putting her name in. [*He looks inquiringly at Madame, who is struck dumb by their brutal rudeness.*] Seems to be hard of hearing. You sound her.

SERVANT. Lot of competition this time, Ma'am, and only a few places left.

MADAME [*nervously*]. It's a very great honour, sir, and my girls are very anxious to go, but our family has no . . . you understand. . . . My husband died without leaving any . . . We are most willing, but . . .

SERVANT. His Honour will not ask you a big fee . . .

MADAME [*murmuring*]. We are so badly off . . . Yet my girls are not bad-looking . . . I thought perhaps . . .

SERVANT [*scandalized*]. Heavens! Ma'am, do you expect us to work for nothing?

CHRYS. Oh, please . . . please . . . [*seeing all her hopes fading and bursting into suppressed sobs.*]

LI [*annoyed, sits down at a table*]. Just as I thought, pure waste of breath with these paupers. Brush and ink! And where is the list?

SERVANT [*handing list and brush and ink*]. Here, sir. [*Pointing at the paper*] And there is the house in Pewter Lane, sir.

LI [*writing*]. What shall I put as reason for rejection?

SERVANT [*looking Chrysanthemum up and down*]. Over-dressed? Over-rouged? Over-powdered? Timid? Nervous? Ill-bred? Stupid? Any of those would do.

[*Madame and Chrysanthemum give a little shriek at each of these words, while Li scrutinizes the paper.*]

LI. I notice on the list there is another girl in this house. Orchid? Where is she? [*Madame looks at him full of hope.*] I'd better have a glance at her . . . [*She brightens appreciably.*] so as to know what word to use for her rejection!

ORCHID [*from inside her room*]. Just put her down as unsuitable, your Honour!

[*This unexpected voice makes the men start. Li looks round the room.*]

LI. A striking voice! Who is that?

MADAME. My daughter . . . Orchid.

LI [*loudly*]. Unsuitable? Of course! But I have to give a definite reason. Come out! I want to have a look at you. Do you think I'm an ogre? What are you hiding for?

ORCHID. I'm not hiding, but I don't want to waste your Honour's time.

SERVANT. Not as timid as the other girl, sir!

LI. Probably so ugly she doesn't want to show herself.

SERVANT. You may be right, sir.

ORCHID [*coming out*]. You may be right, your Honour.

[*Li starts up astonished. With a mocking smile Orchid bends her knee slightly. She is wearing a light green gown, and is without powder or jewellery, her only ornament being the pale green orchid in her hair. But she has calculated rightly; the simplicity of her appearance, contrasting so sharply with her sister's, adds enormously to her natural loveliness. Li and the servant cannot take their eyes off her.*]

And you may be wrong!

SERVANT. Yes, you may be wrong, sir!

LI [*exclaiming*]. Heavens, what a beautiful girl! And what taste in dress!

SERVANT. Certainly she is not over-dressed like her sister, sir.

LI. Nor over-rouged and over-powdered. Sit down, please.

ORCHID. I prefer to stand until the honourable visitor has resumed his chair.

LI. And not ill-bred, either. Thank you. [*He sits down.*]

ORCHID [*taking a seat some distance from the men, but in a calculated and seductive pose*]. You needn't thank me for that. The courtesy was paid not so much to you as to His Majesty, in whose service you have come.

LI [*with an uncomfortable grin*]. Smart! [*to his man*] I perceive we have met our match! [*to Orchid*] Now that I've seen you, it breaks my heart to reject you. But you see, we eunuchs have to live. Isn't there any chance at all of your managing some money . . . ?

ORCHID [*demurely*]. We needn't bother about that! I do not *want* to go.

LI [*staggered*]. What! Do you really *not* want to go into the Palace?

ORCHID: What is the use? If people realized that their own promotion depended on what a favourite might whisper into Imperial ears, one could make a bargain. But as it is what can one do if they are so shortsighted as to prefer a trifling fee in cash.

LI [*thinking*]. A-hem! I can take the hint. But even were I to enter you, it would mean you'd be only one of the Ladies-Constant-in-Waiting who are no more than servants, and most of them remain so until their hair is grey.

ORCHID. You said "most of them". Then there *are* exceptions?

LI. Yes, some may become Imperial Concubines, and rank next to the Empress. That is why this business is generally called the Selection of Imperial Concubines. But not more than two out of over a hundred girls are ever given that rank.

ORCHID. I would like to hear the details. How are they all selected?

LI. I see you are ambitious!

ORCHID [*charmingly*]. Is there any objection to that?

LI. No, on the contrary! Well, our Lord of Ten Thousand Years is to have an Empress, two Imperial Concubines, twelve Lesser Consorts, thirty-two Noble Ladies, and sixty-four Ladies-Constant-in-Waiting. As soon as the girls I select come into the Palace, the Chief Eunuch examines them carefully and the Empress Dowager promotes some of them to the rank of Noble Ladies, leaving sixty-four to be Ladies-Constant-in-Waiting. Later she will pick from among the Noble Ladies some to be promoted as Lesser Consorts.

ORCHID [*rather alarmed*]. And does the Emperor himself have no say in the matter at all?

LI. No, not at first. But not all the vacancies for the Lesser Consorts will be filled at once. As time goes by the Lord of Ten Thousand Years may favour some of the girls and have them promoted. Of course, when the Empress Dowager mounts on high in her Phoenix Carriage, then the Lord of Ten Thousand Years may even name his own Empress.

ORCHID [*thoughtfully*]. How old is the Empress Dowager?

LI. Not very old, though she is getting on. But don't dream, my girl. People from families like yours seldom get promotion. Besides, you must have the eunuchs on your side, and they all have to live.

SERVANT. Yes, sir, they all have to live.

ORCHID. Then, is money everything in the Palace?

LI. I should say that the eunuchs' backing is everything. And you can't get it without paying.

ORCHID. But there are various ways of paying!

SERVANT. His Honour prefers cash down.

ORCHID. I'm curious to know, your Honour, how you managed to get this important mission of selecting the candidates while you are so young? Also by paying cash?

LI. I don't pay. I render services.

ORCHID. That's what I meant. And why couldn't a girl do that?

LI [*grinning*]. I see! Still, can't you raise a little loan somewhere? For instance, the person who recommended you to the Palace. Couldn't he help?

ORCHID. It was Lady Mu-Yang-O, whose daughters got in a couple of years ago and have had such a brilliant success, who put our names up. I don't want to bother her now, for I hope to make use of her in other and more important matters.

LI [*impressed*]. Really, the great Lady Mu-Yang-O! And you've other things in mind! Then after all you have seriously been thinking of getting into the Palace?

[*An idea seems to strike him. He pauses, seems to decide and abandoning his rather jocular manner seats himself close to her and whispers so that the others cannot hear.*]

If I take you and put you under my protection, can I count on you to say nice things to Lady Mu-Yang-O and her daughter, the Imperial Concubine?

ORCHID. No! [*Li looks up in surprise.*] Why should I speak to them when I have a chance to speak to Himself?

LI [*eyes wide open*]. Himself? Are you bold enough to aim so high?

ORCHID. At the sun, if you like.

LI. At the sun! [*The word seems to astonish him.*]

ORCHID. Maybe we are each indispensable to the other. Don't you want to become the Chief Eunuch one day?

LI. How do you know that?

ORCHID. A clever young man like you has his eyes fixed on the horizon. And he knows that a lady's backing is as needful for him as a eunuch's is for her.

LI. Then it is a bargain?

ORCHID. It is.

LI. That I should have believed for a moment you did not want to compete! What a clever actress you are!

ORCHID. Is that a drawback in the palace?

LI. Certainly not! You have to act with everyone, and first of all with his Honour, the Chief Eunuch Hsiao, but I'll put in a good word for you there. We must pray that he will suggest you to the Empress Dowager for the rank of Noble Lady.

ORCHID. It must be Noble Lady. You leave him to me.

LI [grins]. I couldn't leave him in deadlier hands. [Beckoning to Madame] Well, thinking it over, and not wanting to be hard on a lady who is a bit pressed I'll take one of your daughters free this time, if you pay me a double fee next, when I come for the other.

MADAME [overwhelmed with joy]. You are very good, sir.

CHRYS. But suppose there is no next time?

LI [lightly]. Then I lose my tip.

CHRYS [tragically]. And I lose everything. [She begins to sob again.]

LI. Make the necessary preparations, Lady Orchid. [He is grinning, but she is quite calm.] Messengers from the Palace will come in due course with a sedan chair for you. In the meantime we must move on. Good-bye for the present, future Lady Constant-in-Waiting.

ORCHID [with spirit]. Lady Constant-in-Waiting! We'll see about that.

LI [turning to Madame]. It distresses me to have to leave you, Madame. . .

MADAME. Sir, you are too kind.

LI [to the servant]. You tell her!

SERVANT. Ma'am, it is unlucky for us to leave a house without receiving anything, so just as a matter of form could you find a small piece of silver . . . or . . . some little jewel . . . [He looks covertly at Chrysanthemum's jewels and Orchid smiles demurely.]

ORCHID [cruelly]. Little sister, do you hear?

CHRYS [angrily]. Why should I? It's not my business! Besides, they are all brass! Brass! Brass!

[Madame is mortified, and Orchid chuckles. The servant looks askance at Li, who glances round the room and goes slowly towards Chrysanthemum. He suddenly snatches the embroidered cloth from her hands and looks at it coolly.]

LI. Pretty poor stuff, but I'll keep it as a souvenir.

[*He hands it to his servant and they go out. As soon as the men are gone, Chrysanthemum breaks out in loud crying. Both her mother and sister come to her side.*]

MADAME. Don't cry, perhaps it is all for the good. After all, you are still young.

CHRYS. Oh, no! I shall die an old maid!

MADAME. Stop crying. Tears will spoil your lovely face.

ORCHID. No, they will only wash away some of the powder and rouge on it, and it needs a wash badly!

CHRYS. Oh, you selfish pig! You are always for yourself, never caring about your younger sister!

ORCHID [*in her teasing, jocular way*]. You are quite wrong. I always put the family first. I used to wish my father was Emperor. Since he wasn't, I dreamed at least my husband would be. Then I would think, if that were impossible, the next best thing would be a son as Emperor. And failing that—here is where you come in—and failing that, my nephew should be Emperor. And whenever I thought of a nephew, it was always your dear little son, and not any brat that worthless brother of ours might have.

CHRYS [*childishly*]. Oh, thank you, thank you ever so much!

ORCHID. But I'm afraid that was only a dream. As they haven't put you on the list, it's not much good building hopes on your son. So it comes round to this, I shall have to be content with a husband who is Emperor!

CHRYS [*in floods of tears*]. Oh, oh, oh!

ORCHID. Don't be silly. Let us go in and wash this thick paint off your face. Now, stop wriggling. You ought to be proud that a Lady-Constant-in-Waiting's first duty should be to clean you up.

CHRYS. Oh! oh! oh!

[*Orchid and Madame more or less drag her away.*]

END OF SCENE TWO

[Wen Li enters in a pensive mood and says];

The producer of this play gave me his word as an honourable barbarian that nothing derogatory to Her Imperial Majesty should be played. I believed him and felt free during the later rehearsals to visit the eating shops of your disgusting city, where, I confess, I sampled your wines, which, though deplorable concoctions, wrought nevertheless their influence upon this humble person. Taking advantage of my absence, and of my good spirits on return, he has represented the Holy Mother in a light for which the Imperial Histories give no warrant whatsoever. It is inconceivable that She should have intrigued with a eunuch to enter the Palace. His anticipation that such a libel would win your applause proves, I regret to say, how lamentable is your taste. Let me state with all emphasis that the Venerable Ancestor was selected solely on account of Her virtue and high accomplishments.

In the scene now about to be shown you will see Her at the Summer Palace, known as Yuan-Ming-Yuan, the Round Bright Garden, which is outside Peking, and, provided my instructions are carried out, you will be edified by the propriety of Her behaviour, which so attracted the Lord of Ten Thousand Years that he promoted Her from the rank of Noble Lady to that of Lesser Consort.

[He bows stiffly and withdraws.]

SCENE III

(The fourth year of the reign of Hsien Feng, 1854.)

The great Royal Park of Yuan-Ming-Yuan is a landscape of lakes, canals, hillocks, and terraced gardens, white marble bridges and flowering trees. In this park one of the hundreds of pavilions, which are situated at carefully chosen viewpoints, is called the Lacquer Tree Bower. Lofty trees with big evergreen leaves, known as lacquer trees, are planted around it and in the foreground peonies of various colours fill up its courtyard. The main building of the pavilion is to the extreme right and therefore only the back wall with its latticed windows and door can be seen. There is a spacious verandah outside the door, on which are a few bamboo benches and a tea table surrounded by porcelain flower pots planted with orchids in full bloom.

Noble Lady Orchid, wearing no headdress, which means that she is expecting no visitors, appears on the verandah in a light pink loose gown and carrying a round fan. In her black hair, which is coiled into a knot, there appears that symbolic orchid again. A year's easy life in the Palace, especially that of a Noble Lady, is liable to make anyone rather plumper. But Lady Orchid has managed it so well that we begin to feel she has put on just sufficient weight to bring out the curves which are one of her attractions. She is accompanied by a maid.

ORCHID. A poet once remarked that the sun seemed nearer to him than the Imperial Capital, but for me the case is just the reverse. The Palace has been too close for my liking and I begin to feel somewhat confined. However, a year here has improved my painting, and I have had leisure to study the classics and history.

MAID. Yes, Noble Lady.

[*Orchid sits down on a bamboo bench.*]

ORCHID. Bring me the Philosopher Chuang.

MAID. Yes, Noble Lady.

ORCHID. And I'm at home to no callers.

MAID [*going*]. No, Noble Lady.

[*While Orchid is examining the flowers in the porcelain pots, the maid returns with a pile of large books. Putting them on the table and lifting it near to her mistress she tells her of an unexpected caller.*]

Excuse, me Noble Lady, but the doorkeeping eunuch has just said that the Lady Mu-Yang-O's daughter, the Imperial Concubine Niu-Ku-Lu, has sent word to say she is coming. What shall I tell him?

ORCHID [*turning the leaves of a book calmly, but her voice betraying some irritation*]. Haven't I told you often enough there are certain persons whom I must see at any time of the day and that Lady Niu-Ku-Lu is one of them? [*with more control*] Since the recent death of her sister, the Empress-Elect, she is too important to ignore, though, of course, that is not my reason for welcoming her here. Her mother, Lady Mu-Yang-O, is my mother's oldest friend. [*perceiving that the maid is still there*] What are you standing there for? Go at once and ask her to come in.

MAID [*flying away*]. Yes, Noble Lady!

ORCHID. 'Yes, Noble Lady! No, Noble Lady!' A girl like that makes me forget where I got to in my Philosopher last night.

[*She searches impatiently through one volume after another, even tearing the leaves when she cannot find her place.*]

Ah, here it is at last! The dream about the butterfly, of course!

[*Just then the maid reappears and announces the Lady Niu-Ku-Lu, a plump young person full of smiles. She has a round face, is pleasing enough, but quite lacking in character or intelligence. Orchid finds her visits tiresome, for in spite of her good nature, she is a shallow boring woman. She wears full summer court dress, which is black gauze, and a tall satin headdress. She is followed by a maid who stops near the door. She comes forward ingenuously, with total lack of ceremony, in spite of her court clothes, while Orchid rises stiffly and advances formally to meet her, though in the easiest of undress.*]

NIU-KU-LU. Butterfly? Goddess of Mercy! With your big loose sleeves like wings, you mustn't fly away like a butterfly, Orchid!

ORCHID [*smiling mechanically*]. What a happiness to be favoured with your Ladyship's visit. You have news I can see. May I inquire what it is? Pray sit down.

NIU-KU-LU [*rather excited*]. Please dismiss your maid. It is a secret. [*She sits down on a bench opposite her.*]

ORCHID [*waving her hand to maid*]. You can go!

[*They are left alone.*]

NIU-KU-LU. You won't tell anyone?

ORCHID. I have never abused your Ladyship's confidence. But do not keep me in suspense. Your secrets are always so full of interest.

58

[*It would have taken a much cleverer woman than Niu-Ku-Lu to detect the ennui with which Orchid awaits the revelation.*]

NIU-KU-LU. My mother has just told me that the Empress Dowager has just told her that . . . that . . . Goddess of Mercy! She is thinking of nominating me Empress-Elect!

[*Orchid is dumbfounded. She had expected stupid gossip and hears instead that this commonplace girl is to be head of the Court. It is quite a full second before she can regain her presence of mind. Then, she smiles her carefully practised smile and stands up ready to curtsey to the future mistress of the Palace. But Niu-Ku-Lu thinks she is coming to congratulate her, and rushing forward hugs her, uttering a series of happy cries. Her eyes are actually full of tears of happiness.*]

NIU-KU-LU. Oh! Orchid, I knew you would be overjoyed. Isn't it wonderful?

ORCHID [*without a trace of sarcasm*]. Wonderful! [*But disappointment, jealousy and anger convulse her face as she leans on Niu-Ku-Lu's shoulder. She, too, is almost in tears.*]

NIU-KU-LU. Mother was so delighted. We had a good cry together. Besides, it was only the second time I had seen her since coming into the Palace two years ago.

ORCHID. I haven't seen my mother at all since I came in.

NIU-KU-LU [*naïvely*]. But your home was not the same as mine. We were all so comfortable and happy together. My brothers were so nice—I was always sorry about *your* brother.

[*Orchid winces slightly.*]

And there was my dear dear sister, who was to have been Empress. How I miss her!

ORCHID. But you shouldn't. Hasn't her loss been the making of you?

NIU-KU-LU [*her inanity revealing itself*]. Yes, but before she left for the Palace she used to take me out shopping. To tell you the truth, I don't miss her as much as the shops. Goddess of Mercy! you can't buy a thing here.

ORCHID. But everything is provided free. And now, I daresay, you'll get more things free than any of us can hope to get.

NIU-KU-LU. That's just it! There's nothing to spend one's Court allowance on. What's the use of having plenty of money when you can't have the fun of buying anything?

ORCHID. I find my allowance rather tight.

NIU-KU-LU. Of course, you have to support your family.

ORCHID [*nettled*]. I have not sent them a single piece of silver the last six months. My brother Kwei Hsiang has got a job in the Li Kin now, you know, and it pays him well.

NIU-KU-LU. Thanks to his sister, I expect.

[*They resume their seats. Orchid rings a little bell and the maid immediately brings in two bowls with covers and saucers, which she places on the tea-table.*]

ORCHID. Do try my tasteless tea. I'm afraid you will find it nothing like yours. But you must feel thirsty after . . . [*She cannot bring herself to pronounce the words*].

NIU-KU-LU [*drinking like an ox*]. I mustn't . . . drink too much . . . I feel . . . so hot already . . . but I am . . . so thirsty.

[*While she is drinking, the maid approaches Orchid and whispers something in her ear.*]

ORCHID [*with an uneasy glance at her visitor*]. Don't you remember that I told you I am at home to nobody except Lady Niu-Ku-Lu?

NIU-KU-LU. Oh, I'm going anyway. Goddess of Mercy! I'm so hot, I must get back and take off some of my things. Good-bye, Orchid. It was so nice to have a little cry with you. And thank you for your lovely tea. The tea they supply to me is dreadful. I must speak to the eunuch in charge.

ORCHID. Not at all! Your tea, I always think, is quite delicious.

NIU-KU-LU. Do you really? I'm very glad. Oh, Orchid, since you are so kind to me, I wonder if I might send over some of my allowance to you? It is of no use to me and you said you wished yours was more.

ORCHID. No, no, I was only joking. I have no use for the money, either.

NIU-KU-LU. Oh, come, now! I know you are a bit extravagant. I heard the little eunuchs say so. Only they didn't use the word, extravagant. They called you Lady Generous. Good-bye, Lady Generous!

ORCHID. Good-bye. [*Turning to maid when the visitor is out of sight*] Show him in as soon as the path is clear.

MAID [*going with tea things*]. Yes, Noble Lady.

ORCHID. Empress-Elect! What is the Court coming to! I suppose her fat was the chief attraction. And, of course, the Empress Dowager wanted a nonentity.

[*She takes a little mirror from the tea-table and looks at her reflection. She smiles.*]

Wait till I have my chance.

[*She puts the mirror back and picks up a purse, heavy with small pieces of silver. She takes some out and counts them carefully.*]

My mother always said I was a miser with small silver and a spendthrift with big ingots, but she forgot that a mountain is composed simply of bits of earth. I suppose I must have spent a hundred taels in handing out this small silver.

[*The maid brings in a young eunuch and she signals him to approach.*]
What is it?

EUNUCH [*bowing*]. I have a message for the Noble Lady from His Honour Li.

ORCHID [*impatiently*]. Yes?

EUNUCH [*in a low voice*]. The Lord of Ten Thousand Years returned last night.

ORCHID. Ah! [*a pause*] Is that all?

EUNUCH. His Honour ordered me to say there might be further news later.

ORCHID. Very well. Tell him I am pleased. Here is your reward.

[*She throws him a small piece of silver. He takes it and shows he is disappointed.*]

You may go now!

EUNUCH. And I thought the news was extraordinary. The Lord of Ten Thousand Years has not returned to the Park for a very long time.

ORCHID. So you think twenty-five candareen is not enough? All right, here is another ten. Be off, now!

[*She throws another small piece of silver to him. The eunuch pockets it, thanks her, and goes away. Immediately after the maid has seen him out, she brings in an old eunuch. Orchid looks at him in surprise.*]

From whom do you come? You are not sent by Li Lien-Ying, are you?

OLD EUN. No. But I have news to report to the Noble Lady.

ORCHID. Let's hear what it is.

OLD EUN. The Lord of Ten Thousand Years returned . . .

ORCHID [*curtly*]. Yes, returned from the City last night. Everyone knows that. You can go. No tip for that.

OLD EUN. There is another piece of news. His Majesty had melon for breakfast.

ORCHID [*forced to laugh*]. Melon! Melon for breakfast! And you expect a tip?

OLD EUN. It is well known among us that the Noble Lady pays for any news of the Emperor. I listened and watched. How could I tell what was the thing she wanted to know? His Majesty seldom eats melon. It may be a sign of something.

ORCHID. Well, I hope it is.

[*She throws a small piece of silver to him and he shuffles off, thanking her. In the meantime, someone appears near the back gate on the extreme left, and Orchid, not turning her head to see, whispers to the maid.*]

Someone is approaching the back gate. You stand on tiptoe and see who it is.

[*She picks up a volume of Chuang and appears to become immediately absorbed.*]

MAID. It's His Honour, Li Lien-Ying, Noble Lady. Shall I tell him to come by the front gate while you go and change?

ORCHID. No! [*standing up impatiently*] Come straight in, Your Honour.

LI [*approaching the verandah*]. Did you get my message?

ORCHID [*pretending to be less interested than she really is*]. Oh, yes. But does it make much difference where he is? He will never look at us Manchu ladies as long as he has those Chinese prostitutes.

LI [*heaving a sigh*]. Oh! He may tire of them.

ORCHID. He may tire, but there are no signs yet. What is there in the Chinese girls? Their small feet, do you think?

LI [*sagaciously*]. More likely they have some amusing tricks.

ORCHID. Tricks? What sort?

LI [*with a leer*]. Tricks of making love. He's long past the ordinary kind of thing, you know.

ORCHID. Is he? I didn't know.

LI. Oh, yes, you may be sure that is how they amuse him.

ORCHID. Is that the reason they have such a hold on him?

LI. Fairly obvious, I should say.

ORCHID. Thanks for the hint. It may come in useful. Have you any further news for me? What is his programme to-day?

LI. I have a piece of excellent news for you at last, anyhow hopeful news. There's a chance if you play your part.

ORCHID. What is it? I know my part. You may take a seat.

LI. Thank you [*stepping on to the verandah and sitting down*]. When I went in to massage the Emperor as usual this morning, for the first time in many months he said nothing of his Chinese favourites. Instead he began talking about the improvements to the gardens, and told me he wanted to inspect the new Peony Terrace.

ORCHID [*excited*]. The one near here from where I got those flowers?

LI. Yes.

ORCHID. Will he be passing my gate, then?

LI. Yes and no.

ORCHID. What do you exactly mean?

LI. If he takes the shortest cut from his Palace, he is bound to pass this back gate of yours . . . [*He points left.*]

ORCHID [*with an intent look*]. Yes?

LI. And if he does, you won't want him to see you dressed the way you are. He's on the road already. You had better slip indoors.

ORCHID. You think I ought to do that? But what then?

LI. Listen. I have bribed his sedan eunuchs to take a longer route on the way back so that he'll pass your front gate [*pointing right*]. They'll be wanting a short rest after climbing the hill and the shade of the lacquer trees will be just the place for it.

ORCHID. And then will someone suggest he should come in?

LI. No. It must be done more tactfully than that.

ORCHID. I see you have a plan!

LI. It is you who must induce him to come in.

ORCHID. Oh! I have to provide a plan?

LI. It's going to be a collaboration. You play the mandolin, do you not, and very well?

ORCHID. Yes. But so do the Chinese girls. And some of them are professionals. He will not love me because of my music.

LI. It is one thing to hear a mandolin at an entertainment, and another when its notes reach you in a beautiful landscape, as you pass a pavilion set on a hill. Debauched though he is, he is not yet dead to the lure of an adventure.

ORCHID. Perhaps, perhaps. But your plan needs improving. You say he is inspecting the Peony Terrace. Well, I'll play the new popular tune 'Peony Cheeks'. And with these flowers in the court-yard, the coincidence will intrigue him as much as the romance.

LI. You are very clever. He is much guided by such coincidences. But he won't be able to see these peonies from the front.

ORCHID. No. But I'll stop him when he passes the back door.

LI. Not an orthodox way for the Emperor to enter the pavilion of a new lady.

ORCHID. It wasn't in an orthodox way that I entered the Palace.

LI. Well, no! In that case, you have no time to lose in dressing up for the occasion. Quick, he may be passing any moment. I hurried on to warn you.

ORCHID. But I *am* fully dressed for the occasion. If his entrance is unorthodox, everything must be unorthodox. Lovely though my court dresses are, they are not cut to make love in. Perhaps that is the real secret of the Chinese girls. They are not bothered with official dresses. Let me show you what I mean.

[*She kicks off her slippers and leans back, one leg to the ground, one leg on the bench, her gown loosened negligently. Li is quite startled, but shows he agrees, and takes leave hurriedly. She calls after him in high spirits.*]

And I bet you could never tear yourself away from me if you were —if you were—not what you are! [*turning to her maid*] Bring my mandolin to me.

[*She takes up her Philosopher Chuang once more.*]

'How can I be sure that I am really a philosopher dreaming of being a butterfly, and not a butterfly dreaming of being a philosopher?' It was a bit of a puzzle for him, poor Chuang!

[*The maid brings the mandolin to her.*]

Thank you. [*Putting down the book and beginning to play the instrument very softly*] Now dishevel my hair a little more for me. [*Maid does so.*] Do I look wicked enough?

MAID [*automatically*]. Yes, Noble Lady.

ORCHID [*teasing*]. You dare to call me wicked, do you!

MAID [*alarmed*]. No, Noble Lady.

ORCHID. Oh, but I am!

MAID [*miserably confused*]. Yes, Noble Lady.

[*There is a commotion by the back gate.*]

ORCHID. You may go.

[*She alters her position so that anyone looking over the gate will have a good view of what she is taking care to show. She seems to be wholly absorbed in her playing. The tune of 'Peony Cheeks' becomes louder as the Imperial Procession draws near. Soon the upper half of the Yellow Sedan is seen high above its bearers' heads and shoulders, and the Emperor Hsien Feng's voice is heard saying 'Halt!' From the sedan window, he can be seen staring at the attractive musician. But the view from the window isn't good enough, and he wants to get out. 'Down!' he says. The Son of Heaven is not very much to look at, a young man with a prematurely old appearance. He is thin, pale and not very tall. He wears his everyday black dress and a white straw summer court hat with a coral button but without peacock tails. He gets out of the sedan and stands on tiptoe. But he cannot see as well as he*]

咸豐帝

EMPEROR HSIEN FENG
(*Not very much to look at, a young man with a prematurely old
appearance*)

did before. He gets into the sedan again. The bearers think he wants to leave and start to go on.]

HSIEN FENG. No! you fools! Back a little bit! No! Forward! That's right. Don't move now.

[*While he is devouring her with his eyes from the sedan window, the whole procession waits in silence. Li Lien-Ying moves stealthily nearer and watches anxiously.*]

What's that tune? Isn't it 'Peony Cheeks'? Peonies seem plentiful about here, blooming in the courtyard and floating on the air. Reminds one of a picture of the Taoist Paradise.

[*Li hurries up, falls on his knees beside the sedan and says with an ingratiating laugh.*]

LI. The Lord of Ten Thousand Years has a wonderful ear. It is, indeed, 'Peony Cheeks'.

HSIEN FENG [*straining to get a better view*]. Beautiful! Beautiful! But who is the musician?

LI [*getting up*]. May I inquire?

HSIEN FENG. No. No. Don't disturb the music. But who is she, I wonder? And what a charming place! I declare I was quite right to speak of Paradise.

LI. The pavilion is called the Lacquer Tree Bower. Is it the Sacred Wish to enter? Perhaps from inside a better view will be obtainable— a much better view of . . . the garden.

[*He signals to the sedan carriers and opens the gate silently. They lower the sedan and the Emperor gets out once more and comes to the gate.*]

HSIEN FENG. Perhaps, you say?

LI. Certainly, I think. Indeed, I am sure!

HSIEN FENG. You all stop here and wait.

[*He waves his hand to prevent anybody following him and steps into the courtyard. Orchid continues to play as if unaware of the presence of a visitor. He stands looking at her from quite close for a moment, and then goes a step nearer. She turns round, gazes at him in feigned surprise and then, with that grace and animation for which she was to be famous, and which made her irresistible, her eyes full of an overflowing spirit of delight, she gets up and then falls on her knees. Hsien Feng turns to the gate and says loudly to Li.*]

Now, Li, you may inform her of Our presence.

LI [*coming into the courtyard, but remaining near the gate*]. The Lord of Ten Thousand Years deigns to call on you.

ORCHID [*in a tone of mingled gaiety and admiration, to which as a con-*

65   E

summate actress she can give conviction]. Your humble maid, the Noble Lady Orchid, heartily welcomes the Sacred Chariot.

HSIEN FENG. Orchid? I had thought perhaps it would be Peony.

ORCHID. One should mingle the flowers in a nosegay.

HSIEN FENG [*as if under a spell*]. Yet there are some flowers that are most beautiful and, mixed with others, make them seem paltry.

ORCHID. Such flowers are rare.

HSIEN FENG. And when found should be tended. Come.

[*He moves to a bench on the verandah and sits down.*]

ORCHID [*kneeling*]. Your humble maid is not properly attired to receive Your Majesty's favours.

HSIEN FENG [*stretching out his hand to help her up*]. We forgive you for the offence. It is clearly not intended.

ORCHID [*rising*]. Your Majesty has taken me unawares, or else I had not been idling on the verandah.

HSIEN FENG. But I see you have been reading. [*pointing to the books*] Ah, the works of Chuang! What chapter have you got to?

ORCHID. The Philosopher's dream of his being a butterfly.

HSIEN FENG. And wondering whether he was a butterfly dreaming of being a philosopher? What is your solution?

ORCHID. My solution is not to solve it at all. One is happiest just dreaming.

HSIEN FENG. When I heard your melody stealing over the hill, I too fell a-dreaming.

ORCHID. Had I known the Dragon was abroad I might not have dared to send out my notes.

HSIEN FENG. Is the Dragon, then, so very alarming?

ORCHID. We small people are easily afraid.

HSIEN FENG [*putting out a hand, to which Orchid bashfully offers one of hers*]. Beauty has no reason to fear.

ORCHID. Where there is profusion, even beauty will be neglected.

HSIEN FENG [*putting out the other hand, when Orchid demurely offers her other*]. Yet even in profusion the wise man knows how to choose.

[*He rises and walks slowly with her towards the door of the building.*]

Come in and let us follow the example of our philosopher and seek happiness in dreams.

[*She looks at him adoringly and pretends to be extremely reluctant to surrender. Trembling and panting, she says in a low voice.*]

ORCHID. But the Imperial attendants are waiting outside. What shall I tell them?

[*He whispers something and she is joyfully surprised. She makes as if to kneel down but he stops her and says in her ear.*]

HSIEN FENG. You'll tire your legs by kneeling too much! And we need them for other purposes! Give my orders first.

ORCHID [*turning towards Li, who is standing by the gate, and making a covert sign to him*]. His Majesty desires to inspect the Lacquer Tree Bower. Send away the sedan. It will not be required until to-morrow. And issue an announcement that the Noble Lady Orchid is promoted from to-day to the rank of Lesser Consort.

LI [*stunned by her sudden success*]. The Chief Eunuch is on leave. May I point out that I am in the second rank. Only a eunuch of the first rank can act as the Deputy Chief and issue an announcement.

ORCHID [*in a grand manner*]. Kneel down at once to His Majesty for the favour bestowed on you. The Lord of Life is incapable of making a mistake. You have already been promoted!

LI [*kneeling down and kow-towing*]. May the Heavenly Face flourish for ten thousand ten thousand years!

[*Hsien Feng, signalling him to go at once, enters the building followed by Orchid. Li withdraws and the procession retires quietly.*]

END OF SCENE THREE

[*Wen Li enters, looking happier. Maybe he has had another cup or two of wine.*]

When reflecting on the admonitions I have addressed to you, a point occurred to me which I had omitted to make. You should always remember that the Motherly Countenance foresaw Her great destiny and knew it to be essential to the glory of China that She should rise to the Dragon Throne. Now there are innumerable classical precedents to show that the duty of a patriot is to sacrifice all, even his own reputation, for the good of the State. So if—though I do not admit it to be the case—the Auspicious One on occasion saw fit to act in a way unbecoming to ordinary mortals, it may properly be argued that She was bound so to do when thereby She secured more certainly for us the inestimable benefit of Her guiding hand.

Thus, though to represent Her playing Her mandolin with the intention of attracting the Son of Heaven is historically incorrect, for, as is well known, She *happened* to be playing it at the moment he was passing, nevertheless had She done so Her action would have been justified and any resulting loss to Her reputation would have been balanced by Her readiness to sacrifice it for the State.

This principle, if borne in mind, will help you to understand Her motives in the scene which follows. You will remember She is now a Lesser Consort. Her new name is Yi, a word which may be rendered by your poor word, Virtue. That the Lord of Ten Thousand Years should choose for Her such a title sets beyond doubt—if doubt existed—the fact of Her integrity. His Majesty, having no son, we shall now perceive how She sought to supply what was so essential, not for Herself, but for the dynasty.

[*He bows and walks off haughtily.*]

SCENE IV

The bed-chamber in the Lesser Consort Yi's apartments in the Forbidden City is a room remarkable, not only for its beauty, but for its comfort. The occasion being one for celebration, red court lanterns are lit, and early flowers in massive porcelain pots on high stands have brought spring itself into the room. This is lofty and spacious; the walls are panelled and the roof, for the building is of one storey, is supported on lacquered pillars, the beams, too, being lacquered, and carved with designs.

Her Highness's couch, with its green silk curtains and its satin and embroidered quilts of various colours, stands to the right, while to the left is a big chair, the high back carved with a dragon in clouds. This chair is reserved for His Majesty, should he call, and is known as the Dragon Seat. Nearer to the bed is a dressing table and mirror of ebony inlaid with mother-of-pearl. On the table are various cosmetics in porcelain vases and jars, and silver and gold boxes, all of antique design and beautifully made. The honey and perfumes are contained, not in glass bottles, but in small porcelain pots, in shape not unlike miniature tea-pots.

Close to the Dragon Seat is a desk on which are writing papers of various shades; brushes, their holder of white jade carved with pine trees; a fish-shaped ink tablet inscribed with a poem; a brush-support of blue porcelain in the form of mountains; a melon-shaped water-container; and a vase of moon-white for the flower of the month. Within easy reach is a small bookcase, the books bound in flowered silk. On the walls, splendidly mounted, are specimens of Her Highness's calligraphy and painting. It is clear that, besides paying due attention to her appearance, she is not neglecting her mind.

However, an object quite unconnected with either the toilet or the arts occupies an important position. This is a lacquer cradle, and it stands in the middle of the room. Sleeping peacefully in it is an infant, an infant prince who is Heir Apparent of the Chinese Empire, a fact which explains why the cradle is yellow.

The Lesser Consort Yi appears in a purple silk gown, with a turban of the same colour round her head. She is followed by two maids and a nurse. A third maid carries a coverlet.

YI. Millions of babies are born to serve, while only one of them is born to rule.

[*She sits on her couch. The nurse goes to attend the baby and rocks the cradle gently. Two maids take their places on either side of the couch while another spreads the coverlet over the lower part of Yi's body.*]

Send the Grand Physician in. I am ready.

MAID [*retiring*]. Yes, your Excellency.

YI. Put a cushion by the couch for him to kneel on when he takes my pulse.

MAID. Yes, your Excellency.

[*They place a cushion as desired. The Grand Physician enters with his head bent down and keeps his eyes on the ground all the time. The maid leads the way. He is an elderly man with a very discreet appearance. He wears over his gown the official court overcoat with breast pattern, and a court hat with a crystal button. He walks slowly with a peculiar high-stepping gait in case he should commit the rudeness of stumbling over anything, a formality sometimes used in the presence of royalty.*]

PHYSICIAN [*as he comes on*]. For a medical man to have the honour of visiting the Imperial Family is comparable to walking on thin ice. One never knows when will be one's last trip in this world.

[*He follows the maid and kneels on the cushion before Yi's couch and begins to kow-tow.*]

My humble respects to your Excellency.

YI [*putting out her right hand on the arm of the chair*]. You are excused the usual ceremony. Take my pulse.

PHYSICIAN [*stopping kow-tow and taking her pulse*]. A truly remarkable recovery. Let me congratulate your Excellency.

YI [*rallying him*]. To what will you ascribe it in your official report?

PHYSICIAN. To your virtue, Lady.

YI. A proper reason! And to what else?

PHYSICIAN. To my skill, inadequate though it is.

YI. Inadequate? That is the wrong word. Your skill was wholly adequate—for such an easy delivery. But you are right to ascribe it to your skill—skill, that is, in diagnosing the vital needs of the State.

PHYSICIAN. I trust your Excellency is wholly satisfied with me.

YI. I am satisfied—so far. And I think I have shown my satisfaction by the promise of a superintendency of the Li Kin tax for your son and a liberal reward for your services. Nor will that be all [*changing her tone*] provided that . . .

PHYSICIAN [*nervously*]. Pray continue, your Excellency.

70

YI [*giving him a sudden bleak look*]. Need I?

PHYSICIAN [*much shaken*]. No, no, your Excellency. I quite understand. You can wholly rely upon my . . . my discretion.

YI. I hope so . . . for your own sake and for your son's. You may retire without prescribing for me.

PHYSICIAN [*getting up, bowing very low and withdrawing backwards*]. I shall ever treasure your Excellency's gracious words. [*He turns and retires.*]

YI. Tell the Deputy Chief Eunuch, Li Lien-Ying, that I can receive him now.

IST MAID [*going*]. Yes, your Excellency.

YI [*to nurse*]. Take the Prince to the inner room. [*To the two other maids*] Go, all of you, and prepare the bath. See that everything is done before His Majesty arrives.

NURSE AND MAIDS. Yes, your Excellency.

[*They retire with the infant. Immediately after this Li Lien-Ying enters and stands at a little distance, ready to kneel.*]

YI [*signalling him to stop*]. Excused. There is no one about. I've just given the Grand Physician a final warning.

LI. I saw him pass. He looked frightened.

YI. Still, your eunuchs should watch him. Having signed all the prescriptions, he can hardly speak without compromising himself. Nevertheless it is better to be on the safe side.

LI. I will see that your orders are faithfully carried out. But there is no need to worry. Your position is now assured. As mother of the Heir, all power will come to you.

YI. There is that fool of an Empress, Niu-Ku-Lu.

LI [*calmly*]. On the Emperor's death the mother of the new Emperor becomes Empress-Dowager.

YI. The Emperor is young.

LI. But his health is already undermined.

YI. True.

[*She seems to fall into deep thought. Then suddenly, as if awakening from a dream.*]

You are looking too far ahead. The present matter is not quite concluded. The mother of the child has still to be rewarded. Bring her in.

[*Li goes to the entrance and claps his hands three times. A young woman of the people, clad in a grey cotton jacket and a pair of black trousers, enters timidly. Li conducts her in, and she kneels at some distance from the couch.*]

Who is your husband, woman?

WOMAN. I am a widow, your Highness.

YI. Why do you consent to give the child to me?

WOMAN. I was promised a large reward. Who wouldn't for that?

YI. Have you spoken of this to others?

WOMAN. Oh, no, Your Highness!

YI. You will speak of it afterwards, perhaps?

WOMAN. Never! Your Highness forgets that I am a widow.

YI. Very well, you may go.

WOMAN [*hesitatingly*]. Where is the child? May I have a last look at him before I leave?

YI [*coolly*]. No.

WOMAN [*with great feeling*]. As a request from one mother to another—

YI [*surprised*]. What makes you think I am a mother?

[*Li tries to explain. She stops him with a gesture.*]

Let her speak!

WOMAN [*frightened and looking guiltily at Li*]. I hope I have said nothing wrong. But His Honour told me that Your Highness had just lost a new-born Prince—

LI [*in whisper to Yi*]. I thought it better to put it that way to her.

YI [*smiling*]. Very thoughtful of you, Li. Take her to another room. I've got a wonderful reward for her.

[*Li leads her to the entrance and beckons a eunuch to take her away. He then comes back.*]

You think it safe to let that woman go home?

LI. She is very poor. A good reward and she is your devoted slave.

YI. That's just what I have been wondering. Great affairs of state are hardly conducted in that way. No, no, Li. I can take no more risks. It is enough that the Grand Physician knows and lives.

LI. Then you desire me to . . . ?

YI. Yes. When she asked so appealingly to see the . . . the Prince, I knew it would not do. Mother-love in a woman is admirable, but it can be dangerous. . . . For the sake of the State, reward her with this.

[*She produces a long and narrow piece of white silk and hands it to him. Her face is very set. He looks at her with admiration, bows and leaves. As soon as he is gone she summons the nurse and the maids, who come in with the infant. She takes it over from them and tries in various positions to nurse it. The 1st maid hurries in.*]

His Majesty?

MAID [*kneeling*]. Yes.

[*Everybody in the room kneels except Yi. Hsien Feng, followed by two eunuchs, enters the room and signals all to get up. He goes to Yi, while the eunuchs stand at a distance.*]

YI. Excuse your humble maid for being unable to kneel on Your Majesty's arrival.

HSIEN FENG. You are always pardoned now, Yi. [*with an expression affectionate and happy*] How well you look! You are recovered marvellously.

YI. It is because Your Majesty has come to visit me.

HSIEN FENG. I was overjoyed to read the Grand Physician's report. Before, when they told me you had conceived, I could not believe it, you remember, until you convinced me yourself. And then I feared it might be a girl. [*with fervour*] Heaven has been very kind. Those who whispered I had exhausted the Mandate of Heaven were mistaken. My ancestors will thank you.

YI [*who knows when to assert herself*]. *Our* ancestors, may I remind your Majesty. But they should thank you in the first instance. Will you take your son, the Prince, and nurse him?

HSIEN FENG [*awkwardly taking the infant and going back to his chair*]. He is asleep.

YI. Be careful. You will drop him! The likeness is remarkable, is it not? He has your Majesty's ears and chin.

HSIEN FENG [*hypnotized by her*]. Yes, and my nose too. The resemblance is startling. [*Holding child farther away*] But what of his eyes?

YI. Gently, don't waken him! You should see his smile. He has your smile, though perhaps his eyes are more like mine. My mother used to say that as a baby I had rather small eyes.

HSIEN FENG [*believing her*]. Had you? Then he will be clever like you. Has the Imperial Astrologer examined his nativity? What did he say of my son's eight characters?

YI. Exceptionally good. [*To nurse*] Take His Highness. His Majesty has already begun to spoil him, I see.

HSIEN FENG [*giving child to the nurse*]. And you'll drive out the Red Barbarians, the English, the French, and the rest of the foreign devils for your poor father [*making a funny face at the baby*], won't you, my lit-tu Prin-cee?

YI [*solemnly*]. That is certain. And so auspicious a day should be marked in some special manner. Has Your Majesty thought of issuing rewards?

73

HSIEN FENG. Ah yes, rewards. Have you any to suggest?

YI. Well, the Grand Physician. His Mandarinate is only of the fifth grade.

HSIEN FENG. I'll give him leave to wear the button of the third.

YI. Your Majesty is very good. And he has a deserving son— [*coaxingly*]—and I understand a superintendency of Li-Kin tax is vacant at Foo-chow.

HSIEN FENG. If that is so, he shall have the appointment.

YI. During the pregnancy the Magistrate of Nanking, an old friend of my father's, often sent me delicacies of the South. His name is Wu Hui-Chen.

HSIEN FENG. He shall be promoted to a prefecture.

YI. Our son, as you know, has a devoted aunt. My sister, Chrysanthemum, made all the lovely dresses for him. She predicted it would be a Prince and all the clothes are for a boy!

HSIEN FENG. Then she must certainly be included. What do you recommend? Say it and it shall be done.

YI. For a beautiful young girl—a good husband! As your brother, the Prince Chun, is looking for a wife, it would be doing a good service to both to bring them together.

HSIEN FENG. What a brilliant idea! Yes, yes! When one's happy, one wants everybody to be happy.

YI. There'll be the occasion when our son is a month old. Could not a party for them be given that day in Yuan-Ming-Yuan? Its lakes and flowers, what more could lovers want?

HSIEN FENG. Indeed, yes! And we, too, must go boating again. When you are strong enough we shall renew the happy life we led those first few months in the Round Bright Garden. Picnics—boating —plays—music! It will be Heaven!

YI. Your Majesty must not neglect your official duties.

HSIEN FENG. I want a holiday and a rest. The city air is bad for my health.

YI. It would be as well to have the State papers sent to the Garden.

HSIEN FENG. But my ministers will not be in attendance.

YI. They may be ordered to join you.

HSIEN FENG. What! Our holiday will be utterly spoiled! No, I can't have them with me there.

[*An idea strikes him, as she had intended that it should.*]

Besides, it is not necessary. You can advise me better than anybody else. Your proposals in the past have always been most sound. These

74

troubles with the Outer Barbarians and the Tai Ping rebels are causing me much concern. The Grand Council is quite at a loss. You may be able to think of something.

YI. What talents I have are vowed to the State, but I am sure Your Majesty does not need my poor advice. Yet the devotion of a faithful servant can sometimes be an inspiration. Your Majesty may count entirely on mine.

HSIEN FENG [greatly flattered and pleased]. You are too modest. And that reminds me, there is someone else who richly deserves a reward.

YI [pretending not to understand]. Has anyone been left out?

HSIEN FENG [touched]. How unselfish you are! Yourself, of course. You think of everybody except yourself. I now proclaim you the Imperial Concubine, Yi.

YI [forgetting her part for a moment and moving as if to get off the couch and kneel]. I thank Your Majesty—

HSIEN FENG [stopping her with agitation]. No, do not get up. Take care of yourself for my sake [rising] and take care of the boy for the sake of the State. [signing to the eunuchs] I must drag myself away. A pile of mandates are awaiting my seal.

[Everybody except Yi kneels while he passes out of the room with his eunuchs. Li immediately enters with the piece of silk, now somewhat twisted, in his hands. Bowing low, he displays it to Yi.]

LI. It is done.

YI [in formidable voice]. Thus a great empire is preserved.

[They all retire.]

END OF SCENE FOUR

END OF ACT ONE

[Wen Li enters in a rather aggressive mood and says]:

In a famous passage Mencius declares: 'The Superior Man does not argue with birds and beasts.' The Superior Man, however, has always known when to make an exception—and so I have spent the Interval arguing with the Producer. He has found my arguments so helpful to his barbarian mind that he has requested me to repeat some of them to you.

Should any of you have doubted for a moment the propriety of Her Majesty's action in adopting a child and giving its mother an opportunity of showing her loyalty to the State, you will, on reflection, have perceived that She was merely following the Confucian principle which I have already enunciated. But to remove any vestige of doubt in your minds, I will quote you two passages from the Classics. Reverently attend! Mencius said:

'Of the three cardinal sins, to have no descendants is the worst.' And the Master said:

'To achieve goodness, a man should never hesitate to sacrifice his life.'

But I need not labour the point. It must be clear even to the least scholarly amongst you that in Her Majesty's care for the succession She was acting in strict accordance with the classical Books.

Four years have now elapsed. During that period a deplorable event has occurred. The Outer Barbarians—I am speaking particularly of your ancestors, though to use so respectful a term as ancestor is rather a solecism when referring to your hairy progenitors whose sole profession, if I may say so without offence, was trading in opium, piracy and arson—the Red Barbarians, I say, with an effrontery which was truly laughable, petitioned that an Ambassador from their savage island be permitted to reside permanently in our Celestial Capital.

When this petition was rightly rejected, they marched on the Heavenly City and, not content with desecrating the Great Within with the beastly presence of their soldiery, burnt the Summer Palaces of the Yuan-Ming-Yuan. The Son of Heaven found it convenient at this time to inspect his hunting lodge at Jehol, a hundred miles distant. The Imperial Concubine Yi—to use her then title—accompanied him with Her Son, and the important events which you will now see represented took place in that palace in the Province of Manchuria.

[He inclines his head slightly and retires.]

76

ACT TWO
JOINT RULE
SCENE I

(The 16th of the 7th Moon, the eleventh year of the reign of Hsien Feng, August 21st, 1861.)

Though the old Hunting Palace of Jehol is in bad repair, it is a fine lofty building and has recently been redecorated to receive its royal occupants. As the work was done in a great hurry, the place has rather a ragged look. The temporary Imperial Bedchamber is badly and sparsely furnished. Besides the Dragon Bed, there is only a small desk with a few chairs. The hot summer days should have provided the Imperial Household with plenty of flowers but owing to the lack of gardeners only a few pots of common plants are seen.

Following two eunuchs, His Majesty Hsien Feng enters, leaning heavily on the shoulder of a third. Even without the almond yellow silk turban round his head, which indicates that he is not well, anyone can see that he is totally unfit for hunting or any kind of sport. Four or five years of happy life with the Imperial Concubine Yi have left their mark on him, and the Tai Ping Rebellion, together with the Anglo-French invasion, have made his hair turn grey. He wears a plain almond yellow silk gown and black satin shoes. Evidently he has not been out of doors to-day.

HSIEN FENG. With ten thousand State matters waiting to be settled, the life of the Imperial Orphan is not a very enviable one!
[*He takes his seat on the Dragon Bed and begins to glance over various papers piled on his desk. The two eunuchs retire, leaving the other one to wait at his side. None of the papers conveys to him any good news. He shakes his head with a sad expression over one, sighs deeply over another and hurriedly throws down a third. On two of them he has to affix the Imperial Seal, which is a heavy square block of jade, and this proves to be too strenuous a task for his feeble hands. With great difficulty he manages to do one, but for the second he has to ask for help.*]
Come here! Fix the Imperial Seal on this for me.
[*The eunuch hurries forward and seals it for him so deftly that one knows it to be a job he has often done before.*]
I wish my ancestors had had the sense to choose a smaller and

lighter piece of jade for a seal. Didn't they realize one would have to lift it fifty times a day!

[*A third document has to be sealed. He frowns. Enter a eunuch who kneels at a distance.*]

EUNUCH. Her Highness the Imperial Concubine has sent the Grand Physician to wait upon My Lord.

HSIEN FENG. Show him in.

EUNUCH. Yes, my Lord.

[*Hsien Feng continues reading the papers as the eunuch retires and shows in the Grand Physician, who starts to kneel.*]

PHYSICIAN. Your servant the Grand Physician . . .

HSIEN FENG [*waving his hand to stop him*]. Enough! Sit here and examine my pulse while I go on with my work.

[*The Grand Physician sits on the left of the Emperor who puts his left hand on the desk, and the Physician begins to feel the pulse.*]

PHYSICIAN. Your servant risks ten thousand deaths by observing that the Imperial pulse is extremely weak to-day. As he has submitted before, repose is the sovereign remedy for the exhaustion from which Your Majesty suffers. Worry is very bad. All public business should be deferred . . . if possible.

HSIEN FENG. I wish it were possible! Why, even the Imperial Seal is too heavy for me.

PHYSICIAN. I beg Your Majesty not to attempt to lift it for the time being.

[*The Emperor closes his eyes and shakes his head weakly.*]

How does Your Majesty find the medicine I prescribed? The deer's blood is a very effective tonic—and not merely a tonic, for it has strong powers of rejuvenation. But I have informed Her Highness, the Imperial Concubine, as she is looking after the medicine, that an excessive dose may be dangerous . . .

[*He picks up a small bowl with a little gold teaspoon in it. Holding the bowl in his right hand, he tries to show the gold spoon to the Emperor with his left.*]

Your Majesty can safely take it twice a day, but never more than half this full. [*He waves the little teaspoon.*]

HSIEN FENG. It has been very stimulating, indeed rather too violent [*opening his eyes for a moment and seeing the bowl only*]. Oh, yes, I generally take it twice or at most three times a day, and I never exceed half a bowl each time.

[*These words petrify the Grand Physician. He feels himself looking into an abyss. The bowl falls from his hand and crashes into many pieces on the ground. He kneels convulsively.*]

PHYSICIAN. I beg Your Majesty's pardon! It slipped out of my hand.

HSIEN FENG [*with a negligent gesture*]. You are pardoned. But to proceed, I have a feeling that the tonic only helps me to draw my reserve energy in advance. After each dose my spirits run high for a short while and then I generally suffer a relapse.

PHYSICIAN [*getting up*]. Yes . . . yes, Your Majesty . . .

[*He is trembling, and his forehead is covered with perspiration.*]

May . . . may I have Your Majesty's permission to withdraw?

HSIEN FENG [*who has shut his eyes again*]. Don't feel uneasy about the bowl. Yes, you may go.

[*The Grand Physician retires, his face as white as a sheet of paper, and walking, to use a Chinese expression, as if treading on clouds, so treacherous does he feel the ground beneath his feet. When he has gone the eunuch in attendance says*]:

EUNUCH. Her Highness the Imperial Concubine has sent His Honour Li to massage my Lord.

HSIEN FENG [*without opening his eyes*]. Send him in.

EUNUCH [*going*]. Yes, my Lord.

[*Li, who has been waiting at the door, enters. He stands looking towards the Emperor for a second, his face expressionless. Then he advances towards the Dragon Bed. He is carrying a covered dish container in red lacquer which he puts on the desk beside the Imperial Seal. He kneels close to the Dragon Bed and begins to kow-tow. The Emperor opens his eyes for a second.*]

HSIEN FENG. Don't kow-tow, Li. I want my massage badly. I'm very low—no strength left.

LI [*opening the dish container and producing a steaming bowl and a little gold teaspoon*]. Here is Your Majesty's second bowl of deer's blood for the day. Her Highness said Your Majesty should drink it whilst it's still warm. She cooked it herself with bird's-nest [*putting the teaspoon into it*]. With Your Majesty's permission I will taste it first [*taking a spoonful and licking his lips*]. It's delicious!

HSIEN FENG [*looking at him*]. Thank you, Li. I know I can always trust you. [*as Li puts the bowl to his mouth*] It's almost full, but the Grand Physician said I mustn't take more than half a bowl at a time.

LI [*holding the bowl for him*]. No, but it is really less than half a bowl. It's mixed with bird's-nest soup. Your Majesty knows Her Highness is a wonderful cook.

79

HSIEN FENG [*swallowing*]. Em . . . em . . . em . . . It seems thick. Em . . . em . . . em.

LI. It will give your Majesty strength [*putting the bowl down*]. May I massage Your Majesty now?

HSIEN FENG. Yes, yes. [*He lies down on the Bed.*]

LI [*beginning to massage the Emperor's legs and saying to the eunuch in attendance*]. Clear the broken pieces of the bowl away.

[*The eunuch starts to pick them up.*]

HSIEN FENG. I'm stiff! The hurried journey here did me a lot of harm. I should have stayed in Peking. But they all pressed me to go.

LI. They feared for Your Majesty's safety and for the Heir's. The Red Barbarians are savages. Now, will Your Majesty turn over so that I can massage the royal back?

[*The Emperor turns over, and in the meantime the eunuch goes out with the broken bowl, leaving Li alone with his master. While massaging the royal back with one hand, he takes hold of the Imperial Seal with the other and cautiously places it in the dish container which he closes silently. The conversation goes on while he is doing this.*]

HSIEN FENG. They are savages, yes. But was I not bound to die in defence of the Ancestral Altars?

LI. There was no need. The Barbarians will presently go home. When they cannot get an audience, they will lose face and slink away, as Her Highness the Imperial Concubine says.

HSIEN FENG. She is generally right, but these foreign devils act without respect for law or heaven.

[*He turns slightly, and Li, alarmed, massages the back more vigorously.*]

LI. Your Majesty mustn't move while I massage. Her Highness was greatly shocked to hear of the burning of Yuan-Ming-Yuan.

HSIEN FENG. Poor YI! I know how severe a blow it is to her. We have such dear memories of the Park. Our happiest days were spent there.

[*Just as Li has secured the Seal in his dish container, the door-keeper calls out.*]

DOOR-KEEPER. Her Majesty the Empress is here.

HSIEN FENG [*angrily*]. No! Tell Her Majesty to stop bothering me!

DOOR-KEEPER. Yes, my lord.

LI [*who wants to get away*]. Your Majesty, I must beseech you to control your temper. Her Majesty, with all her faults, comes, I am sure, with the best of intentions.

HSIEN FENG [*wavering*]. I am so busy with State papers this morning. . . .

80

LI. Grant her a few moments. Your Majesty can use her call as an opportunity to relax.

HSIEN FENG. Relax, with her in front of me? [*He laughs derisively.*]

LI. Your Majesty is better. How delightful to hear Your Majesty's laugh again!

HSIEN FENG. As a matter of fact, I *am* feeling much better and more energetic. The bowl of deer's blood and your massage have done wonders. Well, tell her to come in. But you go on with the massage. That will give me an excuse for not looking at her silly face.

LI. His Majesty is ready to receive Her Majesty.

DOOR-KEEPER. Yes, your Honour.

HSIEN FENG. You are such a help, Li.

[*Her Majesty Niu-Ku-Lu enters with two maids and two eunuchs. Though she has been the Mother of the Empire for seven years, she is still the amiable and muddle-headed woman we saw in Act I. She has not changed a bit, except that she is even stouter than before. She is wearing her black court dress and headgear and as it is in the height of a hot summer, she carries a fan and keeps fanning herself violently. She goes towards the Bed and starts to kneel. But being stout and wearing a rather stiff court dress, it takes a moment before she can do so, and the Emperor stops her.*]

EMPRESS. Your humble maid pays her respects—

HSIEN FENG [*impatiently*]. All right, all right. Take a seat.

EMPRESS. Thank you, your Majesty.

[*She takes a seat at the extreme right. Evidently she is quite used to this kind of reception, for her happy face is beaming with smiles.*]

I hope I am not disturbing your Majesty's treatment . . .

HSIEN FENG. No! It can go on while you are here. [*There is silence for a moment.*] Well, what have you come for?

EMPRESS [*awkwardly*]. To inquire after your Majesty's health, and . . . and . . .

HSIEN FENG. And what? Out with it! I'm busy.

EMPRESS. Goddess of Mercy! Your Majesty is always busy. But I can wait.

[*She is silent again.*]

HSIEN FENG. For Heaven's sake, what is it?

EMPRESS. Don't lose your temper, your Majesty. You have almost made me forget what it is.

HSIEN FENG. You madden me! Is it an important thing?

EMPRESS. Oh, no! Just an affair of State.

HSIEN FENG. What? Affair of State, and you say it is not important?

EMPRESS. Not exactly, because it is also a family affair.

HSIEN FENG. Family affair? Can't you speak plainly?

EMPRESS. I don't know how to begin. It's so complicated.

HSIEN FENG. You are driving me off my head!

EMPRESS. Yes, I told your secretary, Su Shun, that it would drive your Majesty mad.

HSIEN FENG. For the love of Heaven, say what it is about!

EMPRESS. Goddess of Mercy! It is about the Imperial Concubine Yi.

HSIEN FENG. What about her? Everybody has been worrying me about that girl ever since I've been ill.

EMPRESS. It's your illness. They say your Majesty should look out!

HSIEN FENG. My illness! Why should I look out? You all have talked a lot, but the only person who has helped has been Yi. Why, she herself mixes my medicine for safety.

EMPRESS. That's it! Look out! She may be putting something in your medicine.

HSIEN FENG [*sitting up on the Bed and confronting her*]. What? What do you say?

EMPRESS [*frightened more by his appearance than by his tone*]. Oh, Goddess of Mercy! Your Majesty *has* been poisoned!

[*Indeed, Hsien Feng's face is very peculiar to look at. His cheeks are burning, his eyes are red and his forehead is covered with big drops of perspiration. He stares contemptuously at her.*]

HSIEN FENG. What ridiculous nonsense! I've just had a bowl of tonic which the Imperial Concubine Yi prepared for me and am feeling much better.

EMPRESS. That must be the poison she sent you!

HSIEN FENG. Rubbish! I never take anything without getting it tasted first. Li, how do you feel after taking my tonic?

LI [*smiling*]. I'm feeling splendid, thank you, Your Majesty. May I withdraw now?

HSIEN FENG. You may, Li.

[*Li takes the dish container and goes out.*]

There are so many papers here, and I want to finish them while I am feeling well. A moment ago I couldn't lift the Imperial Seal. Now, I feel I could lift you, and throw you out, if you don't go!

EMPRESS. But I mustn't go until the Grand Secretary, Su Shun, has had his audience with Your Majesty. He wants me to be here.

HSIEN FENG. What? Is he asking for an audience?

82

EMPRESS. No. He was afraid that your Majesty would refuse him, so he came with me and is now waiting in the ante-chamber.

HSIEN FENG. I won't see him.

EMPRESS. That's right. We thought your Majesty would not see him, so their Highnesses the Princes Cheng and Yee have also come . . .

HSIEN FENG [*jumping up from the Dragon Bed and walking about the room in a fury*]. It's a conspiracy! They're ambushing me!

EMPRESS. Yes, they say that in order to prevent some kind of conspiracy, your Majesty must see them . . .

HSIEN FENG [*desperately*]. All right! All right! I'll see anybody if it will help me to get rid of you! [*shouting frantically*] Show them in, all of them, quick!

EMPRESS [*with her usual inconsequence*]. I knew Your Majesty would insist on seeing them, so don't blame me if what they say is displeasing.

[*The three men enter immediately. Prince Yee is tall and thin and about forty. His long face is full of lines. He has smallish eyes which never look straight at you. His mouth curves downwards and renders it impossible for him to smile. Prince Cheng is slightly older, of medium build, and has an angular face. His half brother, Su Shun, is much younger and very stout. He has a round and smooth face, and his eyes seem to start out of their sockets. They are all wearing court dresses and hats and they kneel down some distance from the Emperor, who is seated again on the Bed.*]

YEE. Your slave, Tsai Yuan, the Prince Yee.

CHENG. Your slave, Tuan Hua, the Prince Cheng.

SU. Your slave, Su Shun, the Grand Secretary.

HSIEN FENG [*impatiently*]. Well, gentlemen, I understand you wish to memorialize me on some important affair of State. You may do so, but avoid prolixity, for I am busy.

[*They are somewhat surprised at finding the Emperor so energetic. After consulting among themselves in whispers, the Prince Yee speaks out.*]

YEE. We would not have presumed to seek audience at this time did not Your Majesty's condition give us no option. It is imperative that a mandate appointing Regents be drawn up forthwith, for, though it is our steadfast belief that Your Majesty's indisposition will pass, the absence of such a document would, in the contrary event, throw the country into confusion. The Imperial Heir, being only five years of age . . .

HSIEN FENG. Gentlemen, you have no cause for anxiety at present.

Su. No cause for anxiety? Why, the provinces are upside down, and when Your Majesty goes to West Heaven, the Empire will be ruined! The Tai Ping rebels are all over the country and the Barbarians are more outrageous than ever . . .

HSIEN FENG [*surprised and angry*]. Stop, Su Shun!

Su [*stubbornly*]. I only speak the truth.

CHENG [*very mildly*]. Good counsel, like good medicine, is not always sweet. I request Your Majesty to think over what we have said.

YEE. Think of the Imperial Heir; for his Highness's sake, Your Majesty should take the necessary measures in case . . .

HSIEN FENG [*sarcastically*]. In case I die to-day—perhaps this instant! Do I look like a dying man? I tell you, I am feeling well, wonderfully well. Don't you believe me? Look!

[*He gets up and upsets his desk with a forceful push. Then he kicks and upsets a chair. Everybody is frightened.*]

EMPRESS. Oh, Goddess of Mercy! Goddess of Mercy! I knew he would be upset!

YEE, CHENG and SU [*knocking their heads on the floor*]. Your Majesty, Your Majesty!

HSIEN FENG [*panting and trembling*]. Now, will you believe I've a few days' life in me yet! Go, gentlemen. Leave me alone.

[*He begins to show signs of exhaustion, and sits down heaving on the Dragon Bed. The Princes prepare to leave, but Su Shun stops them.*]

SU. No, as we have gone so far [*loudly*] we had better finish. Your Majesty, we want to memorialize you that Her Highness the Imperial Concubine Yi, if she comes to power, is likely to steer the country into great danger . . .

HSIEN FENG [*hoarsely*]. Su Shun! Do you realize what you are saying?

SU. Yes, Your Majesty, I do.

YEE. Her Highness, being the Mother of the Imperial Heir, will, in due course, become the Empress Dowager, and her influence on the throne will naturally be great. Unless a Regency is appointed in advance, things will go out of control. . . .

SU. If Your Majesty had not listened to Her Highness's advice, the foreign devils would not have burnt the Summer Palace.

HSIEN FENG. How dare you accuse Her Highness! I have profited very much by her counsel.

SU. So much so that Your Majesty had to leave Peking in a hurry.

HSIEN FENG [*trying to get up from the Bed*]. Su Shun, you are a scoundrel! I'll . . . I'll . . .

EMPRESS. Oh, Goddess of Mercy!

CHENG. The Grand Council does not desire to prejudice Your Majesty against Her Highness without certain proof. But it is common knowledge that her influence has had deplorable results. To settle with the Barbarians will now be no easy matter, particularly should Her Highness come into power. As already mentioned, we trust and believe Your Majesty has many years to live. The situation we have sketched is purely hypothetical. But as it is prudent to provide by Mandate for a Regency now, so also will it be prudent to see that its members are fitted to cope with the problems of the moment. We therefore request Your Majesty to give the matter immediate consideration.

[*While the Emperor is listening to this, certain spasms pass over his face, and he now appears to be breathing very heavily.*]

HSIEN FENG [*in a weak voice*]. There is . . . some point . . . in what you . . . you say, but . . . I hardly feel able . . . at this moment . . . to take the matter . . . farther. Draft a Mandate . . . for me . . . to-morrow. Whom . . . would you nominate . . . for the . . . Regency?

SU [*immediately*]. The Imperial Princes Cheng and Yee, of course. They both have the necessary standing and experience.

[*He then looks at Prince Cheng, who takes the hint.*]

CHENG. And what we lack, no doubt Su Shun could supply in his capacity as Grand Secretary.

[*Su Shun then looks at Prince Yee, who nods to show that he understands.*]

YEE. Yes, and of course the President of the Board of War, the President of the Board of Civil Office, the President of the Board of Rites, the Minister of Horses and other Domestic Animals and the Imperial Brother-in-Law, the Grand Councillor, all should be nominated. The eight of us will be capable of coping with anything.

HSIEN FENG. Well . . . insert . . . all those people's . . . names . . . in the draft . . . I can . . . decide . . . when . . . I see . . . see it.

SU. Here is the draft.

CHENG. Aware that Your Majesty must be spared all unnecessary fatigue, we took the precaution of bringing such a Mandate with us and, if Your Majesty has no further nominations, the Imperial Seal may be affixed to it.

HSIEN FENG [*gasping a little*]. You have . . . a draft . . . already? What . . . does . . . it contain?

SU. Precisely what has been agreed.

HSIEN FENG. I . . . feel . . . much . . . worse.

SU. Exactly what I expected would be . . .

YEE [*hurriedly*]. We are deeply grieved to hear it. But that makes it all the more urgent this Mandate be sealed at once. May we help you with the Imperial Seal?

[*Su Shun takes the Mandate and goes near the Bed.*]

SU. Quick, where is the Seal?

HSIEN FENG [*faintly*]. It . . . is . . . on . . . the . . . de . . . desk.

SU. But Your Majesty has knocked down the desk.

[*They begin to search for the Seal all over the room.*]

YEE. Strange, it's not here!

CHENG. It should be here.

SU. Where on earth has it gone!

EMPRESS [*who is also helping to search for it*]. It's not here. I knew something terrible would happen.

SU [*losing his patience and beginning to throw things about*]. No! Not here definitely! Where have you put it?

[*Getting no reply, he goes to the Bed and sees that the Emperor has become unconscious. Alarmed, he bends over him.*]

Your Majesty! Your Majesty! [*to eunuchs*] Get the Grand Physician!

[*Two eunuchs run out and many run in. The Emperor is still breathing, but the end is clearly at hand. They all rush to the Bed and the Empress starts to wail.*]

EMPRESS. Oh, Goddess of Mercy! Goddess of Mercy! I knew something dreadful would happen!

SU. Curse him! It would be just like him to die leaving the Mandate unsealed!

[*While there is general confusion in the room, the Princes Cheng and Yee, and Su Shun, gather in one corner to hold a conference in whispers.*]

CHENG. Do you think he has been poisoned?

YEE. I don't know. He has been very low recently.

SU. He looks strange. Perhaps the person who stole the Imperial Seal poisoned him!

CHENG *and* YEE. Who?

SU. The Imperial Concubine Yi, of course!

CHENG. It's a serious allegation!

YEE. We must have evidence.

SU. The Emperor was acting in a strange way just a moment ago.

CHENG. That might be 'the Last Bright Rays Just Before the Sunset'.

YEE. We must wait for the Grand Physician's diagnosis.

SU. In the meantime, we should proclaim the Regency at once. We can declare this to be an Imperial Mandate.

YEE. But it's not sealed.

SU. We must risk that for the moment. The Seal can be affixed later, when it's found.

CHENG. Anyway His Majesty agreed to it in the presence of the Empress.

SU [contemptuously]. The Empress! Pooh! We must take the matter entirely into our own hands. She is no match for the Imperial Concubine.

YEE. If we could only get enough evidence to accuse that woman of poisoning the Emperor!

SU. Ah, here comes the quack! I'll speak to him.

[The Grand Physician enters and evidently he is a scared man. Su Shun confronts him, and he trembles more.]

Listen here, your Excellency, we have grave suspicions about His Majesty's sudden collapse. I wonder whether you've had anything to do with it . . .

PHYSICIAN [aghast]. Oh, no . . your Highness, N . . No!

SU [threateningly]. Then maybe somebody else has! Examine His Majesty carefully and tell us the truth. [shouting] The truth, I say!

PHYSICIAN [utterly cowed and going to the Bed]. Yes, your Highness.

[He has a reluctant look at the Emperor, who is now stone dead, and says in a high ritual voice.]

The Emperor has mounted the Dragon!

[There is consternation. The Empress breaks out in fresh wailing.]

SU. And the cause of His Majesty's death?

PHYSICIAN [livid with fright]. I declare . . . that His Majesty . . . has died . . . died of . . .

SU [fiercely]. Go on!

YI [from the entrance]. Yes, pray continue! I am most anxious to hear from his Excellency the Grand Physician what is the cause of His Majesty's sudden death!

[The Imperial Concubine Yi enters in full court dress followed by Li Lien-Ying with rolls of paper in his hand; two maids and four other eunuchs accompany them. Erect and dignified, she glances at the Empress, crouched by the death-bed, her headgear in disorder, her rouged face smudged with tears. There is complete silence. Every head is turned towards his late Majesty's favourite. To the Grand Physician she appears as terrible as an *apparition. He stands with his mouth open, his eyes staring in terror. She looks steadily at him.*]

Go on, your Excellency, finish your announcement!

PHYSICIAN [*nearly in a state of collapse*]. . . . died . . . of . . . of died . . . a . . . natural . . . death . . . your . . . Highness!

YI [*sternly*]. Thank you, your Excellency, you may now retire.

[*The Grand Physician walks off unsteadily. Su Shun glares at him, murmuring with suppressed wrath.*]

SU. What a rat! [*To Cheng*] Now we must proclaim the Regency. [*Giving the paper to him*] Read it!

CHENG [*trembling*]. I feel a bit shaken. [*to Yee*] You had better read it.

YEE [*taking the paper reluctantly*]. I . . . I'll . . . try. [*finding that his hands are shaking*] No, Su Shun . . .you . . . must . . .

SU [*snatching the paper from him contemptuously*]. Where's your nerve gone? What a pair! I'll do it. . . . But this official stuff is a bit difficult to read out.

CHENG. I'll help you.

[*By this time the Imperial Concubine has occupied a seat opposite the Empress near the Bed and Li is standing close behind her. Her maids are by her side and her eunuchs have taken various prominent positions. Su Shun fixes his eyes on her and announces in a loud voice.*]

SU. Before ascending to Heaven, His Majesty gave us this, his last Mandate [*holding up his draft*]. Kneel while I read the sacred words.

[*Everybody kneels and Su Shun starts to read.*]

'In view of Our de . . . de . . . ''

CHENG [*in a whisper*]. Declining.

SU [*continuing*]. 'de-declining health We have seen fit to pro . . . pro . . .'

CHENG [*promptly*]. Provide.

SU. 'pro-provide for a Regency and hereby declare that in the event of Our death, and that during the min . . . min . . .'

CHENG [*softly*]. Minority.

SU. What?

CHENG [*louder*]. Minority!

SU. Oh, yes, minority . . . 'minority of our son, Tsai Chun, the following Princes and Ministers shall act as members of the Committee of Regency: Tsai Yuan, the Prince Yee, Tuan Hua, the Prince Cheng, Su Shun, the Grand Secretary, Mu Yin, the President of the Board of War, Kwan Yuan, the Second Vice President of the

88

Board of Civil Office, Tu Han, the Acting First Vice-President of the Board of Rites . . . '

[*By this time the Imperial Concubine is on her feet again.*]

'. . . Chiao Yu Yin, the Junior Minister of Horses and Other Domestic Animals and Chin Shao, the Imperial Brother-in-law and Grand Counsellor. Respect this!'

YI [*sarcastically*]. Ha! Respect this! It is a bogus Mandate.

SU [*to Cheng and Yee*]. We must assert our authority as Regents at once.

CHENG [*to Yi*]. Your Highness has received with disrespect the sacred commands of his late Majesty.

YEE [*to Yi*]. Your Highness has committed a capital offence.

SU [*to the eunuchs*]. I command you to arrest the Imperial Concubine Yi!

YI [*waving aside the eunuchs who have got up and are approaching her*]. Stop! I repeat that the Mandate Su Shun has read is bogus. It is unsealed. Do you deny this, Su Shun?

CHENG [*whispering hoarsely to Su Shun*]. Don't parley with her or we are lost.

YEE. Order the eunuchs to drag her away.

SU [*shouting at the top of his voice*]. Conduct the Imperial Concubine at once to the Palace prison!

[*The eunuchs hesitate as the Imperial Concubine's eunuchs look fiercely at them. Su Shun is desperate.*]

Go on, you fools!

YI [*in a terrible voice to the eunuchs*]. Stand off! My person is unapproachable! [*to Su Shun*] As your Excellency has not condescended to answer my question, I will now ask Her Majesty the Empress to inspect your Mandate and declare whether it is sealed or not. [*to the Empress*] Your Majesty, if you please.

EMPRESS. Oh, my Goddess of Mercy! I know it is not sealed!

YI [*with crushing politeness*]. Nevertheless, will your Imperial Majesty be pleased to ascertain by inspection whether the paper in Su Shun's hand bears the impress of the Imperial Seal?

[*Su Shun unconsciously passes the paper to Prince Cheng, who again passes it to Prince Yee.*]

EMPRESS. Oh, dear, dear, everyone seems so excited! Show me the paper, your Highness.

[*She stretches out her hand, and Prince Yee, all assurance gone, hands it to her. She glances over it and shows it to Yi and the others.*]

As I have said, there's no seal, Yi.

YI [*elaborately*]. I am vastly obliged. [*to others*] Her Imperial Majesty has declared the paper you have just heard read by Su Shun to be worthless. But here is a genuine Mandate which I will now read to you. Kneel, all of you, and hear the authentic commands of the Son of Heaven!

[*She stands up and motions to Li, who gives her a paper. Everyone kneels while she reads in the high stylized voice used for Imperial Mandates.*]

'In view of Our declining health We have seen fit to provide for a Regency and hereby declare that in the event of Our death, Niu-Ku-Lu, the Empress-Mother, hereafter to be styled Tzu An, the Motherly and Restful Empress and Dowager, and the Imperial Concubine Yi, the Sacred Mother, hereafter to be styled Tzu Hsi, the Motherly and Auspicious Empress and Dowager, shall act as co-Regents during the minority of Our son, Tsai Chun. Respect this!' A Myriad Years!

ALL. A Myriad Years!

EMPRESS. Oh, Goddess of Mercy! I'm to be co-Regent!

SU [*gathering his courage*]. It is impossible that these should be His Majesty's commands.

YI. It is impossible that they should be otherwise, for he has sealed them.

[*She holds up the Mandate upon which is seen clearly the great vermilion impression of the Imperial Seal.*]

SU. As Grand Secretary, I declare that no such Mandate has been drafted.

YI. You are no longer the Grand Secretary. Here is the first Mandate by the new Emperor.

[*She takes a second paper from Li and reads.*]

'Respecting the wish of the co-Regents, their Majesties the Empress-Mother Tzu An, the Motherly and Restful, and the Sacred Mother Tzu Hsi, the Motherly and Auspicious, We feel it Our first duty to deal with the conspiracy which has just been revealed. Taking advantage of Our extreme youth and Our political inexperience, the Imperial Princes Cheng and Yee, and Su Shun, the Grand Secretary, have conspired to usurp Our power. Their behaviour displays a monstrous ingratitude for his late Majesty's favours. We hereby remove them from all their titles and offices. But to show Our leniency, we do not propose to probe further into the matter and readily forgive all those who have blindly followed these three ringleaders. Respect this!' A Myriad Years!

ALL. A Myriad Years!

EMPRESS. Don't blame me for it, Su Shun!

SU [to his comrades]. Let's be gone. [bitterly] If you had listened to me earlier, and done away with the woman, this would not have happened!

[They rise from their knees and begin to slink out when Yi stops them with a gesture.]

YI. One moment! There is a further Mandate. Kneel again while I read it.

[She takes a third paper from Li and reads.]

'Respecting the wish of the co-Regents, their Majesties the Empress-Mother Tzu An, the Motherly and Restful, and the Sacred Mother, Tzu Hsi, the Motherly and Auspicious, We declare that had the conspiracy been no more than an intrigue which was discovered before any action was taken, the leniency to which We are naturally inclined would have prompted Us to dismiss the conspirators without further punishment. But in their attempt to hoodwink Us, they have dared to forge an Imperial Mandate. To overlook this would be an offence to the memory of Our departed Father. We therefore order the arrest of the Princes Yee and Cheng, and the Grand Secretary, Su Shun, and the trial of them on that capital charge. Respect this!' A Myriad Years!

ALL. A Myriad Years!

[She signs to the eunuchs to seize the three grandees and they are taken away immediately. The Empress is bewildered.]

EMPRESS. Oh, Goddess of Mercy! How did you do it, Yi?

YI [with dignity]. Do any further orders occur to Your Majesty?

EMPRESS. Oh . . . oh . . . no!

YI. The Audience is at an end.

[She retires at a stately, slow pace, followed by the others.]

END OF SCENE ONE

[*Wen Li enters and says with a smile*]:

I have just had another friendly argument with the Producer. Even though devotion to the State, I told him, admittedly governed every action of the Benign Countenance, nevertheless it would be advisable, I urged, to stress Her sense of propriety also, and not, as he has done, to depend wholly on the other to justify what might appear to require justification. For a hairy Barbarian he has much amiability and in reply submitted with respect that were he to lay the emphasis I suggested on propriety, the larger part of the audience would quit the theatre. He confessed that in these wild Outer Regions there existed such admiration for boldness that Her Majesty would actually lose face were She shown to be, rather, actuated by virtue. Now, my sole duty is to preserve Her Majesty's face, and if I can do so best by allowing Her to be represented in the light which is here considered the more attractive, however apparently improper that may be, my right course is clearly to grant that permission.

Bearing this in mind I invite you now to consider the next scene. Eleven years have elapsed. The Red Barbarians have withdrawn their troops and though their Ambassadors are now permitted to reside in Peking, their obnoxious presence has been completely ignored. The co-Regents, Tzu An and Tzu Hsi, known as the Eastern and Western Empresses Dowager, have been watching over the young Emperor, who, generally called by his reign title, Tung Chih, has just reached early manhood. They now have an important duty to perform and you will see with what propriety they carried it out.

[*He bows amiably and retires.*]

SCENE II

(The eleventh year of the reign of Tung Chih, 1872.)

The residence of the Western Dowager, Tzu Hsi, in the Purple Forbidden City. Called the Palace of Mind Culture, it is not one of the biggest but is one of the best buildings in the imperial enceinte. The particular room where the following incident takes place is lofty and well decorated. Tall, massive, red-lacquered pillars stand in the four corners. It is a place used by Her Majesty for giving private audience to the inner members of her court. Therefore, except for a few chairs, one or two tea tables, and many big porcelain pots planted with various kinds of trees and flowers, we can scarcely see any furniture at all. It is the early part of a warm spring; the young leaves on the trees are yellowish green, and the flowers are bursting into bud.

Her Majesty Tzu Hsi, the Motherly and Auspicious, is now thirty-seven years of age. When she enters, followed by Li Lien-Ying, now the Chief Eunuch, and other eunuchs and maids of honour, it is hard to believe that she has been directing the Empire for eleven years. Far from being motherly in appearance as her title suggests, she has still a beauty comparable to the opening buds of the flowers around her.

Tzu Hsi. Overburdened with the duties of a ruler and a mother, middle-age is upon you before you've had a moment to enjoy your youth. [*She sits down and frowns.*]

Li. Your Majesty is depressed?

Tzu Hsi [*fondling a blossom not yet fully open*]. Supposing you had stretched out your hand to pick this hardly opened flower and I told you it was faded and should be thrown away, what would you say?

Li. I should say Your Majesty was quite right, for the Holy Mother is incapable of making a mistake.

Tzu Hsi [*laughing in spite of herself*]. Ha ha! Poor Li, you misunderstand me! Supposing I were to tell you that your time was up, and that you must yield your place to a subordinate, how would you feel?

Li. I should feel grateful to Your Majesty, for no doubt my lucky subordinate would be the better man.

Tzu Hsi [*laughing again*]. I call that real loyalty! Ha ha! Aren't you a little slow to-day? Ha ha! But you are making me laugh and I must thank you for that. I haven't laughed this long time. But come, now!

Don't you see my point?

LI. If I am dense, at least it has amused Your Majesty. But what is the matter? Your Majesty is worried?

TZU HSI [*heaving a deep sigh*]. Alas! Li, people begin to think that my days are over. They look for my retirement.

LI. But the Holy Mother will never retire.

TZU HSI. I don't know about that. The Regency cannot last much longer.

LI. I am told that the Eastern Empress Dowager is looking forward to her retirement. She talks of taking up Buddhism.

TZU HSI. She is an imbecile.

LI. Quite so, Your Majesty.

TZU HSI. Have you heard anyone say that of me?

LI. Say it and live? No, Your Majesty.

TZU HSI. Nevertheless, were I altogether to retire when the young Emperor assumes charge, I might be called an imbecile by anybody, I suppose, for it would be true, and safe to say it. Yet to give up and still to hold on is no easy thing.

LI. But for the Holy Mother there always are ways.

TZU HSI. There are many ways. But to select the right one!

LI. Your Majesty's choice is always right.

[*A eunuch comes in and stops at the door to call out.*]

EUNUCH. His Excellency, Jung Lu, vice-captain of the Imperial Guard, has returned to report on his mission and is awaiting the Sacred Word.

[*Tzu Hsi inclines her head and Li says aloud.*]

LI. Let His Excellency come in.

[*Jung Lu is a handsome man of about thirty, tall and dignified among his subordinates, but cringing and humble before Tzu Hsi and other dignitaries. He wears his military uniform, which consists of a red riding jacket, red trousers and skirt and black satin high boots. The button on his hat is of crystal, i.e. of the fifth rank. He approaches Tzu Hsi and kneels.*]

JUNG LU. Your slave, Jung Lu, has returned to report—

TZU HSI [*stopping him*]. All right, nephew, you may get up and take a chair. The occasion is informal.

[*Jung Lu makes a show of refusing the chair.*]

Obey me!

JUNG LU [*sitting down*]. Thank you, Your Majesty.

TZU HSI. I am ready to hear your report.

JUNG LU. I took Your Majesty's birthday presents to His Royal

Highness the Prince Chun's residence and was received in state by their Highnesses the Prince and his Consort, Your Majesty's sister; they both knelt to receive Your Majesty's presents to their baby son.

Tzu Hsi. And how is my nephew?

Jung Lu. The Imperial Nephew is a fine child. His Highness already can walk.

Tzu Hsi. And did he like the toys?

Jung Lu. He cried when I showed them to him. But a baby of a year old, what does he understand?

Tzu Hsi [*frowning*]. Perhaps he was frightened by your uniform.

Jung Lu. Perhaps. But he must have seen others in uniform before . . .

Tzu Hsi [*changing the subject*]. No matter—tell me, how did you conduct your inquiries?

Jung Lu. I sounded everybody there, and that means all the important people in the Capital.

Tzu Hsi. What is the general feeling? What do they think of the Regency's delay in handing over power to the Emperor?

Jung Lu. Your Majesty is too clever a woman to wish me to flatter. I will state the bare truth.

Tzu Hsi. Go on.

Jung Lu. The young Emperor has his admirers. They compare him to a bud about to burst into flower, a glorious flowering . . .

Tzu Hsi [*indignantly*]. And me, I suppose, to a fading flower which at best was blighted.

Jung Lu. No, Your Majesty. I only perceived that there was impatience.

Tzu Hsi. They all want me to go? I know it! I wonder what they see in the boy.

Jung Lu. Your Majesty, historical precedent is on his side.

Tzu Hsi. H'm! I thought as much. Further postponement will only be imprudent. Would you say that the Regency was actually unpopular?

Jung Lu. If it were composed of one person instead of two and that one person were Your Majesty, there could be no question of unpopularity, only regret that the State was soon to lose a guiding hand. But the Eastern Empress Dowager's lack of all administrative capacity has brought it into disrepute.

Tzu Hsi. No one could be more tired of her than I am. To sit in audience opposite that stupid woman, hear her silly exclamations of 'Goddess of Mercy!' and childish questions when she feels she ought to assert herself, and then, before an Edict can go out, be obliged to obtain her counter assent . . . Oh, I do not know how I have borne it all these eleven years!

JUNG LU. But, Your Majesty, with the end of the Regency she will be eliminated.

TZU HSI. Yes, she must go, no matter what happens.

JUNG LU. Precisely so, Your Majesty. There will be no need for her in future to have any share, whilst, if a suitable Consort for the young Emperor is chosen, Your Majesty's power will be largely undiminished.

TZU HSI. That brings me to a point I want to discuss, the sort of girl who will make a suitable consort.

JUNG LU. No one is more competent than Your Majesty to make a judicious choice.

TZU HSI. You are inclined to flatter too much, Jung Lu. It is a fault I dislike intensely.

JUNG LU. But everyone knows that Your Majesty is the only person in the world who cannot be flattered!

TZU HSI [pleased at the compliment]. I see through it, I suppose. But to return to the point—what is your idea of the right consort for the young Emperor?

JUNG LU. Well, to begin with, she ought to be very pretty, very smart, too, and very clever; indeed, someone rather like Your Majesty, though it would be impossible to find your equal in this world. The prettier, smarter, cleverer she is, the quicker the young Emperor will take to her. And that's important, as he can't be forced at seventeen.

TZU HSI. True. But it is extremely difficult to find such a person. There is one of my Maids-of-Honour who might do. I have had her in mind for some time. Will you give me your honest and frank opinion about her?

JUNG LU. Who is she?

TZU HSI. Phoenix Elegance.

JUNG LU. I confess I've never heard of her.

TZU HSI. There, you see, is one of her drawbacks. Her father has only recently been promoted to the rank of a Vice-Minister. They belong to a family which, alas, is not considered one of the best, though I think it is one of the nicest.

JUNG LU. I knew Your Majesty's choice would be judicious. One chooses one's instruments not only for their merits, but also for their shortcomings. A girl of too noble birth would tend to be insufficiently grateful to Your Majesty for her promotion.

TZU HSI [*non-committally*]. I'm glad you can see that. Now, another thing. She is what you would call too young for the post of Mother of the Empire. She is not more than fourteen.

JUNG LU. There, again, I cannot but admire Your Majesty's discernment. Fourteen is the ideal age to ensure of her being completely amenable to Your Majesty.

TZU HSI [*thoroughly pleased*]. Jung Lu, I think you show a great deal of sense.

JUNG LU [*getting down from his chair at once and kneeling*]. What sense I have is always at Your Majesty's disposal. But if my official rank were higher, I should be better placed to serve you. [*pointing to his crystal button*] Though on Your Majesty's service, I was the only person of the fifth rank at the Prince Chun's palace. Most of those present had coral or at least sapphire buttons.

TZU HSI. You have my leave to wear the blue one.

JUNG LU [*again kow-towing*]. A myriad thanks, Your Majesty.

[*A eunuch comes in and stops at the door to call out.*]

EUNUCH. Her Majesty, the Eastern Empress Dowager is approaching the Palace in . . . in . . . at an extremely quick pace! May we know Your Majesty's Sacred Word?

TZU HSI. What a nuisance that woman is! I don't want to see her.

EUNUCH. Yes, Your Majesty.

JUNG LU. One moment! May I suggest that as her consent will be necessary to the appointment of the Consort, it is a good opportunity to broach the subject. She must have something urgent to ask of you, or she wouldn't be in such a hurry. It will be policy to grant it and put her in a good humour.

TZU HSI. Well, I will see her. Meanwhile you may go.

[*She signs to the eunuch. While Jung Lu, after making his bow, withdraws on one side, Tzu An, the Eastern Empress Dowager, enters from the other, followed by eunuchs and maids, who stop outside the entrance. On this occasion she is wearing everyday clothes and is without her high headdress. If in her youth Tzu Hsi looked well so attired, Tzu An, approaching middle age, grown much stouter and inclined to be untidy, is not a pleasant sight. Moreover, her round amiable face, though still good-natured, has coarsened, and her innocent expression, once not unattractive, has become irredeemably stupid. Add, that at the moment she appears*]

greatly agitated, never an assistance to anyone's looks, and we can under-
stand that she is likely to be the occasion less of amusement than of irrita-
tion. She addresses herself to Tzu Hsi without any preliminaries.]

TZU AN. Goddess of Mercy! My little Dragon Eyes is ill again.

TZU HSI. You don't say so? The Imperial dog is unwell? How very distressing! Take a seat and tell me what I can do for Your Majesty, or rather, for Your Majesty's dear little dog.

TZU AN. No, thank you, I couldn't bear to sit about here while poor Dragon Eyes is suffering. [*sitting down*] Oh, my poor dear!

TZU HSI. I quite understand Your Majesty's feelings.

TZU AN. He was in great pain all the night, whining and shaking his poor little head incessantly.

TZU HSI. Poor little soul!

TZU AN. I was so upset. I rushed across as quickly as I could when I remembered you had some powder—

TZU HSI [*puzzled*]. Powder? As I do not keep dogs, I hardly think I have anything suitable.

TZU AN. I know, but when I saw my dog shaking his head in pain, I thought of the awful headache you had the other day, just after sitting with me in audience, you remember, and you took some fine red powder which you said was called the 'Powder of Eight Treasures' and was presented to you by his Excellency, Wu Hui-Chen, the Viceroy of Szechuan.

TZU HSI [*astounded, but controlling her annoyance*]. Oh, yes, I remember now.

TZU AN. Well, will you be so kind as to allow my poor Dragon Eyes to share some of your powder?

TZU HSI [*unexpectedly*]. Share? Why, you can have all of it. [*to Li*] Li, you know the stuff, don't you? It's in a little carved white jade bottle in the left top drawer of my desk. Go and fetch it at once.

LI [*going*]. Yes, Your Majesty.

TZU AN. This is very generous of you. And all of it? Are you sure you won't be wanting it again?

TZU HSI. No, it does me no good.

TZU AN [*surprised*]. No good? But you said it was a sure cure. Won't it cure my dog?

TZU HSI. Of course it will. But it doesn't happen to agree with . . . er . . . my constitution.

TZU AN. I wonder if it will agree with my Dragon Eyes' constitution.

Tzu Hsi. Don't you worry. It will. He has a much better chance than I have.

Tzu An. How's that?

Tzu Hsi. Because your Dragon Eyes need not get up early in the morning to sit in audience with a . . . with a . . . [*controlling herself*] a sore throat and a cold.

Tzu An. No! That's true. Goddess of Mercy! I did not realize you have been suffering from a cold.

[*Li reappears with the little bottle.*]

Ah, here is the powder. Thank you, Li, and thank you, Your Majesty. If you'll excuse me, I'll run along . . .

Tzu Hsi [*stopping her with a gesture*]. Let Li take it over while Your Majesty rests here for a moment . . .

Tzu An. No, thank you. I cannot keep my little darling waiting. I must run.

Tzu Hsi. But surely Li can run much faster than Your Majesty? Li, run with the bottle as quick as you can.

Li [*going*]. Yes, Your Majesty.

Tzu Hsi. Now that Your Majesty is here, there is a matter I may as well mention.

Tzu An. Not State business, I hope. I can't be bothered with affairs of State while my poor dear Dragon Eyes is suffering . . .

Tzu Hsi. Oh no, something which will interest Your Majesty. The Emperor's marriage.

Tzu An [*cheering up*]. How exciting! Yes, I should like to discuss that. You know, I've been looking forward to the day when there is a little one to call me Grandma. Goddess of Mercy! How nice to be a Grandma!

Tzu Hsi. To be a Grandmother you must have a daughter-in-law first. Has Your Majesty thought of anyone?

Tzu An [*unexpectedly*]. Of course I have!

Tzu Hsi [*surprised*]. Really? Who?

Tzu An. That sweet little A-Lu-Té.

Tzu Hsi. A-Lu-Té? I don't know her.

Tzu An. You ought to. She is His Grace Duke Chung Yee's daughter. Excellent family, you see. And, as we want her to be a mother in the shortest possible time, she is not too young, about nineteen. She has a good deal of character, and so can be a real help to the Emperor. And she is a thoroughly good girl, who'll stand by him. I've just made her my Maid of Honour and she is now in the ante-room. Would you like to see her, for I think she is the very person? When we retire, the Emperor will need someone reliable like that.

Tzu Hsi. Chung Yee's daughter? I think I do know her. No doubt there is something to be said for her, but I have somebody much better.

Tzu An (*in a complaining tone*). I think you might sometimes let me have my way, just for a change. In affairs of State I always have to give in to you.

Tzu Hsi. The appointment of an Empress is an affair of State.

Tzu An. But you said just now it wasn't! Oh! this is the only time I've ever pressed a thing. Can't you give in to me just this once?

Tzu Hsi. I don't see why I should. I decided some time ago to have my Maid of Honour, Phoenix Elegance.

Tzu An. That girl! Goddess of Mercy! Why, she's only fourteen!

Tzu Hsi. As the Emperor is not quite sixteen, she is just about right for him.

Tzu An. Not quite sixteen? Why, by next year he'll be eighteen! When shall I be a Grandma with a girl of fourteen as my daughter-in-law? At fourteen I was still asking my poor dear mother where I came from. And I used to ask my poor father why . . . why . . .

[*She looks round, and stops on seeing Tzu Hsi's sarcastic smile.*]

Tzu Hsi. Your Majesty need not tell us what you wanted to know at that age. Nowadays, girls are different.

Tzu An. I realize that to-day young girls know much more than we did. But still, a mere child of fourteen is no use . . .

Tzu Hsi [*quite unused to opposition from Tzu An, finally loses her temper*]. She'll be ten times more useful than your A-Lu-Té.

[*A eunuch comes in and stops at the door to call out.*]

Eunuch. His Majesty the Emperor has come to pay his respects to Your Majesties and is awaiting the Sacred Word.

Tzu Hsi. Conduct His Majesty in.

[*The Emperor Tung Chih enters, followed by his eunuchs who stop at the entrance. He looks much younger than his age, though he has a dignified and grave manner. He wears full court dress and a coral button.*]

Tung Chih [*as he kneels*]. My profound respects to the Empress Mother and the Sacred Mother.

Tzu Hsi. Take a seat, my boy. You've come at the right time.

Tzu An. Yes, in time to settle our difference and back me up. You have always been very considerate.

Tung Chih. Thank you, Your Majesties. [*sitting down on a chair put between them*] I am at Your Majesties' command.

EMPEROR TUNG CHIH

(*He has a dignified and grave manner*)

Tzu Hsi. We have been discussing a matter which has been under consideration for some time, and which has to be settled before you take charge of the Government.

Tung Chih. May I know what the matter is?

Tzu An. Why, the appointment of your Empress, of course!

Tzu Hsi. Among various candidates, I have selected a very suitable young lady . . .

Tzu An. No! Two young ladies, and one not so suitable.

Tung Chih. One not so suitable? What does that mean?

Tzu An [bluntly]. I like one and she likes the other.

Tzu Hsi. Now that you are here and we are discussing this question, I'll tell Lady Phoenix Elegance, who is my choice, to pay her respects to you and, let us say, present you with tea and refreshments. You'll see how proper and charming is her air and how graceful and perfect are her movements. She'll make a most dutiful Empress, as you will perceive.

Tzu An. My choice is the sweet little A-Lu-Té. She is here too. When she comes in, you'll see for yourself what a nice girl she is.

Tung Chih. I'd like to see both of them, but one at a time, don't you think?

Tzu Hsi [to a maid]. Order Lady Phoenix Elegance to come and pay her respects to the Emperor, and in the meantime get tea ready.

Maid [going]. Yes, Your Majesty.

Tung Chih. This will be rather embarrassing for me. I really do not know what to say to them.

Tzu An. And the girls will be shy, too. Goddess of Mercy! If I were asked to do such a thing, I'd be sure not to know how to behave myself. Poor sweet little A-Lu-Té! You'll understand she is young and timid, won't you?

Tzu Hsi. But Your Majesty said just now that she was not too young. However, Lady Phoenix Elegance won't be shy, and she knows how to behave. Ah! here she comes.

[Lady Phoenix Elegance, who enters with graceful steps, is an extremely beautiful girl with a self-possessed air, very smartly dressed in an embroidered red gown. Her willow-leaf shaped eyebrows, her almond shaped eyes and her cherry-like mouth are all so perfect that they look as if painted by a master artist. Above all she has such a charming, demure smile that we agree with Jung Lu in thinking that the boy Emperor will take to her at once.]

Phoenix [kneeling]. Your humble slave girl, Phoenix Elegance, presents her respects to Your Majesties.

Tung Chih [*uncomfortably*]. Thank you. We give you leave to rise.
[*She rises. In the meantime a maid enters with a small tray on which are two porcelain dishes and a bowl of tea. Phoenix Elegance turns to take over the tray. So far her expression and manner are as exquisite as Tzu Hsi has led us to expect. Then suddenly the maid, perhaps because she is a little nervous, slips and falls, and the tray drops on the floor, when we perceive this graceful lady turn in a flash into a little tigress. Her elegant eyebrows and eyes slant upwards and her rosy cheeks are a palish blue. Suffused with anger, she hisses.*]

Phoenix. Look what you have done, you fool! You have not only spoiled my dress, but ruined everything. How can I now present myself before His Majesty?
[*She is in tears and almost ready to kick the poor maid at her feet who is shaking with fright as she picks up the broken things. Then trying to control herself and see what to do, Phoenix Elegance is overcome with fury and breaks into loud sobbings.*]
You clumsy idiot! You . . . Oh! . . . Oh!

Tung Chih. We give you leave to retire.
[*But Phoenix Elegance is too upset to hear.*]
Conduct her ladyship to her room to change.
[*Two maids drag her away. Tung Chih turns to Tzu Hsi.*]
How unfortunate! One is sorry for the girl.

Tzu Hsi [*quite collected*]. You could hardly expect anything else in the circumstances. However, since I planned this little test, it had better go on.
[*She is seen to whisper to a maid beside her.*]
With Your Majesty's permission, we'll summon the Lady A-Lu-Té. [*to maid*] Now, go.

Maid. Yes, Your Majesty.

Tzu An. Hadn't we better postpone it all till another day when Phoenix Elegance has recovered? It won't seem a fair test to His Majesty.

Tzu Hsi. On the contrary, let us settle it once and for all. Ah, here comes the Lady A-Lu-Té!
[*Lady A-Lu-Té is not a siren like Phoenix Elegance, yet she is a very beautiful girl. She seems less of an actress than the other, more natural, better bred, more intelligent and less self-conscious. Though she feels the interview is embarrassing, her dignity enables her to conceal her shyness. She has a gentle candid look in her eyes.*]

A-Lu-Te [*kneeling*]. Your humble maid presents her respects.

Tung Chih [*immediately much taken with her*]. Thank you. [*He seems to become fascinated, murmuring again*] Thank you.

[*The maid enters with a tray as before and Tzu Hsi is obliged to rouse the Emperor.*]

TZU HSI. Will Your Majesty please . . Ahem! . . .

TUNG CHIH [*awkwardly*]. Oh, yes! We give you leave to rise.

[*A-Lu-Té rises. The maid goes up to her and while handing over the tray, slips and falls. She acts her part so well that if we had not noticed Tzu Hsi's whisper to her we might think there was a very slippery spot on the floor. She upsets the tea over A-Lu-Té's dress, and lies on the ground pretending to sob.*]

TZU AN [*staring*]. Oh! Goddess of Mercy! Goddess of Mercy!

[*A-Lu-Té is startled for an instant, but almost at once shows concern for the maid.*]

A-LU-TE. Dear me! Have you hurt yourself?

MAID. I turned my ankle. [*She pretends to try to get up.*]

A-LU-TE. I'm so sorry! Let me help you. [*She bends and helps the maid to get up.*]

MAID [*with well-simulated contrition*]. I've spoiled your ladyship's dress. Now you'll have to serve His Majesty in a soiled dress.

A-LU-TE. No matter. It's not your fault. Lean on my arm. Their Majesties will excuse me while I help you to the ante-chamber.

TUNG CHIH [*delighted*]. Certainly! We grant your ladyship leave to act as you think best!

A-LU-TE. Thank you, Your Majesty.

[*A-Lu-Té and the limping maid retire.*]

TUNG CHIH. That was really remarkable. We could never have thought of such a good test of manners and character.

TZU AN [*beaming*]. I said she was perfect.

TUNG CHIH. She has everything that is important in a wife and an Empress.

TZU AN. I was sure you would think that.

TUNG CHIH [*after a pause*]. Well, Your Majesties asked for my opinion, but I think there is no need for me to say anything further.

[*Tzu Hsi is too angry to reply.*]

TZU AN [*with an innocent, genial smile*]. This is the first time I have ever had my way! Now, we shall see!

TZU HSI [*between her teeth*]. Yes, we'll see!

TUNG CHIH [*with a narrow look at Tzu Hsi*]. Yes, we will see!

[*Tzu Hsi rises to retire followed by the others.*]

END OF SCENE TWO

103

[*Wen Li enters and says*]:

In spite of the Emperor Tung Chih's obstinacy in insisting on the appointment of the unsuitable A-Lu-Té as Empress against his Mother's wishes—a most unfilial act—She entrusted to him the power of the State. We can sympathize with Her anxieties. It was hardly to be hoped that a young man, who had shown such a disregard for the voice of age and experience, would be able to direct the administration of an Empire. Yet, mindful of the laws and usages of China, She resigned the Regency, trusting that he would continue, for a time at least, to come to Her for advice and guidance. But he wilfully pursued his own courses until, at the end of two years, it was evident that She must interfere in the overriding interests of the State.

Such is the light in which you should regard the great Dowager in the next scene—a Mother eager that Her Son should administer the Goodly Heritage as it had been administered by the former Sons of Heaven, and a Ruler who, when She saw dangers threatening it through the disregard of Her counsel, smothered Her maternal instincts and acted with pristine virtue.

[*He retires.*]

SCENE III

(The 5th of the 12th Moon, the thirteenth year of the reign of Tung Chih, January 12th, 1875.)

The Palace of Mind Culture, Her Majesty, Tzu Hsi's, residence in the Forbidden City, has a west wing known as the Western Warm Pavilion, a name misleading in winter, for it is a chilly place. The Pavilion is a lofty hall, generally used for informal audiences, and is extremely difficult to heat, especially when a north wind is blowing, as was the case on January the 12th, 1875. To reduce the draught in that part of the hall which is being used for the moment as a bedroom for the Emperor Tung Chih, a thick wadded curtain is drawn down it, which has the effect of turning the hall into two rooms, to the left being the bedchamber and to the right an ante-room. The Emperor is convalescing after an attack of smallpox, and the Empress-Dowager, prompted, let us suppose, by her maternal love, has caused him to be installed in this wing of her palace, so as to be able to look after him the better. The bedroom is bare and cheerless, hardly better than a prison, the furniture consisting only of a bed, a small table and a few chairs. The ante-room is equally bare. The only decoration is a few prunus shrubs, dwarf pines and cedars. Lanterns are lighted as it is evening. Wearing an almond yellow turban and a blue everyday gown, the Emperor appears, attended by his confidential eunuch, Ma Tang.

TUNG CHIH. The old Emperor Yao was in the habit of saying: 'If anyone in the Empire blunders, the Emperor alone is to blame; and if the Emperor himself blunders, no one else can be blamed for it.'[*He sits down and sighs deeply.*]

MA TANG. Your Majesty should not give way to depression. Moreover, I have this moment received good news.

TUNG CHIH. What is it?

MA TANG. The Empress has sent word to say that she is coming...

TUNG CHIH [*overjoyed*]. Really? But I thought my mother would never allow it!

MA TANG. Her Majesty is coming disguised, as was done last time.

TUNG CHIH [*greatly worried*]. She is running a great risk. This is not my own Palace. How are you going to get her in? Through the ante-room?

MA TANG. No, through the little room behind [*pointing left*] and the secret door there.

TUNG CHIH. Then you had better go and wait at the outer entrance.

[*Ma Tang passes through the curtains and crosses the ante-room. As he reaches the main door, a figure in mantle and hood enters. Taking it to be the Empress, he kneels.*]

MA TANG. Your Majesty has come safely! The Emperor is anxiously awaiting you.

PHOENIX [*throwing back her hood*]. Please inform His Majesty that it is not the Empress, but only his devoted slave, the Imperial Concubine, Phoenix Elegance.

[*Ma Tang is taken aback and cannot find words to answer her. He gets up and is obliged to usher her into the bedchamber.*]

MA TANG. Ahem! Her Highness the Imperial Concubine has arrived!

[*With her demure smile, Phoenix Elegance takes off her hood and mantle and hands them to Ma Tang. She is wearing a beautifully embroidered gown and has decorated her hair with artificial flowers. But these artifices are wasted on Tung Chih, who looks at her in dismay.*]

PHOENIX. Your little maid, Phoenix Elegance, pays her respects to Your Majesty.

[*With a bewitching glance at him, she goes forward slowly and kneels down, hoping that he will stop her and help her to get up. But he makes no move, his face expressing strong aversion and some alarm. Still smiling, she approaches him with a great show of candour and sympathy.*]

Is Your Majesty better? The Empress Dowager has been so anxious. She sent me to inquire.

TUNG CHIH [*coldly*]. I am much better, thank you.

PHOENIX [*the siren in her expression and manner*]. The smallpox has left no marks. Your Majesty's face is as handsome as ever.

TUNG CHIH [*signalling to Ma Tung to go back to the outer entrance and warn the Empress*]. Er ... er ... I had the disease very lightly.

PHOENIX [*archly*]. Your Majesty would not have caught it at all had you remembered the saying: 'Don't pluck wild flowers on the roadside when you have a lovely plum tree in your own garden.' If Your Majesty had sent for your little maid instead of seeking adventures in the Chinese City, all would have been well.

[*Ma Tang manages to slip away during this speech.*]

TUNG CHIH. Oh! Who said that I had been to the Chinese City?

PHOENIX [*indulgently*]. Why, everybody knows that!

TUNG CHIH [*sullenly*]. It is no concern of yours where I go.

PHOENIX [*trying to bring him round*]. Of course not, but if Your Majesty had not gone, perhaps . . . perhaps . . . you would have sent for me, now wouldn't you?

TUNG CHIH [*with irritation*]. I should not have sent for you in any case! I have no intention of being forced. You were appointed Imperial Concubine, not by me, but by the Empress Dowager. Then she stopped the Empress coming to me and thought that would make me send for you. But I preferred to see what I could find in the Chinese City rather than have somebody I didn't want.

PHOENIX [*beginning to lose her temper*]. What a compliment to me!

[*Ma Tang returns and slips into the bedroom. Standing behind Phoenix Elegance's back, he makes urgent gestures to the Emperor to tell him that the Empress has arrived. Phoenix Elegance notices that the Emperor's attention is being distracted and turns about to see what is causing it. Ma Tang has to assume an impassive attitude immediately. However, she seems to guess what is going on and suppressing her anger, becomes plaintive.*]

When making my toilet before coming, I hoped Your Majesty would have a few kind words for me.

[*While she was looking at Ma Tang, the Emperor signalled to him that the Empress must not be ushered in. As she turns back to him, he too has to assume an impassive attitude. In the meantime, Ma Tang is active again. He signs to the Emperor that the Empress is waiting in the back room to the left, and that Phoenix Elegance must be got rid of as soon as possible. She is saying archly:*]

I put on this embroidered gown specially for Your Majesty. Don't you like it? Let me display it better.

[*Like a mannequin, she stretches her arms and lifts her legs, turning slowly round, while Ma Tang and the Emperor's signals continue alternately. It must be admitted that she is exceedingly alluring, but her efforts only agitate Tung Chih the more.*]

It was made by the Empress Dowager's special embroiderers. Would Your Majesty like me to take it off for you to examine closely? Ma Tang, come and help me to undress.

TUNG CHIH. Stop!

PHOENIX [*in a teasing voice*]. Your Majesty needn't be alarmed. I have something under it.

TUNG CHIH [*with cold fury*]. If you have no further message, you may withdraw. Ma Tang, conduct Her Highness out immediately.

PHOENIX. Your Majesty is displeased. Very well! Your slave will not stay where she is unwelcome.

[*She looks vindictively at him and accompanied by Ma Tang passes through the curtains into the ante-chamber towards the entrance. As soon as she has left the inner chamber, the Emperor hurries to the secret door at the back, opens it and stretches his arms to welcome A-Lu-Té, now Her Majesty the Empress, her title being Chia Shun. She wears a dark blue satin gown and is wrapped in a black mantle and hood which she takes off and gives to the Emperor. He carries them away to put on a chair and finds to his dismay that Phoenix Elegance's mantle and hood are still in the room.*

In the meantime, Phoenix Elegance, in the ante-chamber, suddenly turns back before reaching the exit. With a cunning smile on her lips, she makes straight for the inner chamber. Ma Tang, realizing what will happen if she is not stopped in time, retreats quickly and bars the way. She looks threateningly at him.]

Get out of my way, Ma Tang! I left my mantle and hood inside.

MA TANG. I'll get them for Your Highness.

[*But he dare not move. He knows well that if he goes, she will follow him. They stare at each other for a second in silence and then, overcome with rage, she slaps him fiercely on the face.*]

PHOENIX. There! Now get out of my way!

[*At this critical moment, the Emperor comes out with the red mantle and hood through the curtains. He looks angrily at Phoenix Elegance and addresses her in a stern voice.*]

TUNG CHIH. Here are your things. Behave yourself and leave at once.

PHOENIX [*going to him and smiling insidiously*]. Yes, Your Majesty. I *am* going. But may I put on the hood before the mirror in Your Majesty's room? I don't want to disarrange my hair. People think things of a young girl who returns from a visit with her hair in disorder.

TUNG CHIH. Leave at once, I say!

PHOENIX. Very well. Will Your Majesty be pleased to put it on for me?

[*She goes close up to him and he puts on the hood and mantle without looking at her. As he does so she sniffs ostentatiously.*]

Ah! I smell perfume!

TUNG CHIH. Go, or I'll order Ma Tang to drag you away!

[*Ma Tang edges up, ready to take hold of her. She realizes that she can trifle with the Emperor no longer and goes slowly towards the entrance. Tung Chih signals to Ma Tang to follow her.*]

Ma Tang, see that Her Highness gets out of here safely.

PHOENIX [*turning at the door, and in a tone of the utmost impertinence*]. No, it is not perfume. It stinks! Perhaps there is a prostitute hidden in the room, and that's why Your Majesty is so anxious to be rid of me! [*She gives him a knowing impudent look.*]

TUNG CHIH [*provoked beyond all bearing*]. Oh!

[*He is going to rush at her, but a hand comes through the curtains and is laid on his shoulder. Hustled by Ma Tang, Phoenix Elegance now goes. The Emperor withdraws into the inner room, and takes the Empress's hands gently.*]

I might have killed her if you had not stopped me!

CHIA SHUN. Don't bother about her any more. . . . Tell me, are you better? . . . It is such a long time. . . .

TUNG CHIH [*with feeling*]. Yes, two months since that private meeting in my Palace. But how did you manage to get here to-night? Why, the whole corps of eunuchs acts as the Empress Dowager's secret police, and with her nephew, Jung Lu, now Captain of the Imperial Guard, these apartments are as difficult to enter as a prison!

CHIA SHUN. To think of the Son of Heaven . . . a prisoner . . .

TUNG CHIH. Practically so. I can only see persons the Empress Dowager allows to come. Those of the Council who might back me, she would never permit to pass the gates. I often wondered why her men had not penetrated my disguise when I went to the Chinese City, but Phoenix Elegance let out just now that it was an open secret.

CHIA SHUN. Yes, I'm sure the Empress Dowager was told, but chose not to interfere.

TUNG CHIH. What made her not?

CHIA SHUN. Perhaps she was not sorry you ran the risk of catching a dangerous disease. Or maybe she took the opportunity to arrange something more dangerous still. Ma Tang told me that one night you were attacked on the way home.

TUNG CHIH. But those were robbers.

CHIA SHUN. I heard they were Li Lien-Ying's men in disguise.

TUNG CHIH [*with a shudder*]. Then we are surrounded by hidden dangers!

109

CHIA SHUN. Indeed we are! If you think that just because she is amusing herself with those depraved actors, artists and musicians, she is not keeping a close watch on us, you are mistaken.

TUNG CHIH. I wonder how long we can continue these secret meetings.

CHIA SHUN. But that we have secretly met can no longer be kept secret. Everybody will soon know.

TUNG CHIH [alarmed]. How is that?

CHIA SHUN. Because the Empress Dowager's object in keeping us apart has failed. That is what I have risked everything to come to tell you.

TUNG CHIH [with hope and delight in his face]. You mean you are . . . ?

CHIA SHUN [with a touching gesture]. There is a child coming.

TUNG CHIH. This is great news! Why, if it is a boy, you will be Mother of the Heir! Then our troubles will be over!

[At this moment the Empress Dowager Tzu Hsi, in a plain black satin gown and without a hat, appears in the ante-chamber. An outer door eunuch of the Emperor's household rushes forward and, opening his mouth, is about to announce her presence, but with an imperious gesture she commands him to be silent. Li Yien-Ying, who is immediately behind her, takes hold of him and hands him over to a number of burly attendants who are farther behind. Tzu Hsi removes her shoes and gives them to Li. She silently advances in her stockings until she reaches the curtain, only a few feet from the Emperor and Empress inside. Her face is terrifying. Entirely oblivious of her presence, they continue to talk.]

Yes! You will be the most important woman at Court, and everything will be changed. [murmuring] I have been so unhappy.

CHIA SHUN. Just a little patience and everything will come right.

TUNG CHIH. We can hope now. Our day is coming.

CHIA SHUN. Then you can do all the things you have planned.

TUNG CHIH. You also must look ahead. Look forward to the day when you have taken her place, and we can cleanse this dark court, dismiss its ruffians and let in the light.

[Tzu Hsi, whose anger has been rising, is convulsed with rage by this reference to her displacement, though, not having heard the earlier part of the conversation, she is ignorant of the grounds for the Emperor's remark. She stalks through the curtains into the inner room and in a loud, jeering voice addresses the Empress.]

TZU HSI. So you are planning to take my place, are you? You have dared to come and plot with the Emperor at night! It seems I did well to forbid you two to meet, for the moment you are together you conspire against me!

CHIA SHUN [*alarmed but dignified*]. The Emperor and the Empress cannot conspire.

TZU HSI [*sneering*]. Empress! That is a fine title, but it doesn't impress me. [*to Li, in a terrible voice*] Where are the bamboos? Bring them and beat her!

[*Li signs to two of his eunuchs, who step forward with some heavy bamboo sticks. The Empress raises her head with cold indignation.*]

CHIA SHUN. Stop! You cannot beat me. And you know that you cannot, for you are well versed in the dynastic laws. A woman like you, who entered the Palace by a side door and was promoted from servitude, may be beaten, but the Emperor inducted me direct, after I had, in rightful procession, passed through the Great Pure Gate to the Purple City.

[*At this reference to her inferior origin, Tzu Hsi loses all control and with a savage hiss, strikes the Empress straight in the face.*]

TZU HSI. H . . . eh!

CHIA SHUN [*frigidly*]. You forget yourself!

[*Tzu Hsi is momentarily taken aback, and ashamed at her loss of control in the presence of the Emperor and eunuchs, for she knows that for her to strike the Empress is a vulgar act, inconsistent with her position. Profiting by this moment of hesitation, the Empress withdraws with dignity from the room, Tzu Hsi making no attempt to stop her. When she has gone, Tzu Hsi turns on the Emperor a menacing eye.*]

TUNG CHIH. Do not be angry, Mother. A-Lu-Té is innocent of any plot against you.

TZU HSI. I heard! I heard! 'After you have taken her place——' those were your own words to her.

TUNG CHIH. You do not understand, Mother. Those words referred to no plot. We were talking about another matter.

TZU HSI. You were talking of displacing me, that I heard.

TUNG CHIH. Not displacement, Mother. Only the natural legal change that comes with time and the increase of the family.

TZU HSI [*giving him a startled look, but speaking more mildly*]. An increase in the family?

TUNG CHIH [*having no conception that he is signing his own death warrant*]. Yes, Mother, you are going to be a Grandmother.

TZU HSI [*faintly, to herself*]. A Grandmother! I see!

[*Saying these words, all Tzu Hsi's violence leaves her and she becomes perfectly calm, as she always does in the face of danger. She sees, with her wonted clarity, that the news which the Emperor has innocently given means her ruin and probably her death. She begins to pace the room, Li treading in her steps, an expression of eager yearning on his brutal face, for a smell of death gladdens his nostrils. Once or twice she stops, turns and peers at him, slowly moving her head up and down. He knows she is about to strike and awaits her signal, his tongue flickering over his lips as he looks at her with adoration. When she has carefully weighed her decision and thought out her future course of action, she stops, raises her arm and, pointing to Tung Chih, says in an even, slow voice:]*

Arrest the Emperor!

[Li jerks his head at his myrmidons. Two of them rush forward and seize the Emperor who, with dignity, raises his head.]

TUNG CHIH. Do not touch me! You may lead the way.

TZU HSI *[with murderous frigidity]*. Off with him! I do not wish to see him again!

[Sandwiched between Li's men, the Emperor leaves the room in silence, with a look of defiance at his mother.]

LI. And now, Holy Mother?

[He kneels in front of her in a kind of worshipping ecstasy. Tzu Hsi, in the midst of action, always feels a release of the spirit. She sits down and smiles at him.]

TZU HSI. And now, my poor Li? Haven't you been with me long enough to guess? Well, then, take another lesson in how great affairs of State are conducted. The first thing is, of course, to get my court dress and hat.

[Li looks puzzled but obeys her command without question. He jerks his head, and a eunuch leaves the room.]

Then issue orders summoning the Inner Council immediately.

[Li seems to be able to understand this step more clearly and readily gives the order. Another eunuch goes off.]

And last of all, send for His Excellency, Jung Lu, Captain of the Imperial Guard.

[This decree meets with Li's hearty approval. He grins.]

LI. Yes, Your Majesty.

[He gives the order as before, and a third eunuch hurriedly leaves the room. Tzu Hsi looks playfully at him.]

TZU HSI. Now, supposing you were conducting this affair, Li, what would you say to the Councillors when they appear?

LI. Only the Holy Mother knows what should be said.

TZU HSI. Let me help you, Li. As the Emperor is not here, my first statement must relate to him. Now, what should I say about the Son of Heaven?

LI. That His Majesty attempted to poison the Motherly and Auspicious?

TZU HSI. No, no, Li. How stupid you are! I am more concerned about his health than mine. I must speak of his illness.

LI [still mystified]. Yes, Almighty?

TZU HSI. Then I say that he suddenly took a turn for the worse.

LI [beginning to hope]. To be sure! That he became much worse. And then?

[He moistens his lips in anticipation.]

TZU HSI. So much worse, why, that he died, of course!

LI [kow-towing]. So that Your Majesty may be speaking the literal truth, it seems that an order is still required.

TZU HSI. Have you not issued the order? Surely it was implied when I said I did not wish to see him again.

LI. If Your Majesty will excuse me, I will go and make sure that my men understand.

[He withdraws backwards, his face excited and happy, and at the door turns and hastens out. In the meantime Tzu Hsi's court dress and hat have arrived and two eunuchs help her to put them on. While she is dressing Jung Lu enters the ante-room in uniform, now wearing his blue button.]

JUNG LU. Your slave, Jung Lu, reports . . .

TZU HSI [in a loud and authoritative voice]. Attend, Jung Lu! [Jung Lu immediately kneels in the ante-chamber] I have summoned the Inner Council in urgent session for reasons which will be made public later on. The members will be arriving at any moment. Order the commanders of the Imperial Guard at all the Palace Gates not to allow any of the Council members to leave without my permission. No one else on any plea is to enter the precincts, and strict watch is to be kept for disaffected persons. You yourself, from time to time, should enter and report on the measures you are taking. Do you understand?

JUNG LU. I do, Your Majesty.

TZU HSI. Then go at once!

JUNG LU [getting up and going out]. Yes, Your Majesty.

[Li comes in again and grins.]

LI. All Your Majesty's orders have been carried out. The Eastern

Empress Dowager has already arrived and the members of the Inner Council are awaiting your Sacred Word kneeling outside the building.

TZU HSI. Remove the curtain and clear the room for the Council. Show Her Majesty the Eastern Empress Dowager in first.

[*While the eunuchs are busy clearing the room, Tzu An is ushered in. She has put on her court dress in a great hurry and is quite a sight. She comes lumbering up, looking about her in her usual confused manner.*]

TZU AN. What do you want me at this time of the evening for?

TZU HSI [*who is now putting on her headdress*]. Help me to put my hat straight. These men will never be able to do it properly.

TZU AN [*approaching hurriedly*]. Oh! Goddess of Mercy! Is that what you wanted me to come for?

TZU HSI. Yes, but there is another reason. As you are ex-officio member of the Inner Council, your presence is indispensable. Now will you please sit opposite to me on that chair. The occasion is formal and the Councillors will kneel.

TZU AN. Goddess of Mercy! You say the occasion is formal? [*sitting down on the chair and perceiving the room is different*] Why, the curtains are gone! Where is the Emperor? And oughtn't I to know what the business is?

TZU HSI. No need of that. Li, ask His Highness Yi Hsin, the Prince Kung, to lead all the Councillors in.

LI [*who is at the entrance*]. Yes, Your Majesty. [*calling aloud*] Your Highnesses, Your Excellencies, all arise, if you please!

[*A procession of some twenty men, the Imperial Princes and other members of the Inner Council, all in court dress, file in, led by Prince Kung, a wizened little man with a wisp of a beard. They kneel in three rows before the two Empress Dowagers. As they take their positions they announce their names. This would be a tedious business if it were allowed to follow its full course. But as Tzu Hsi is more anxious to get it over than anybody else, she cuts the ceremony short after the first few have announced themselves.*]

KUNG. Your slave, Yi Hsin, the Prince Kung.

CHUN. Your slave, Yi Fan, the Prince Chun.

TUN. Your slave, Yi Chung, the Prince Tun.

FU. Your slave, Yi Fei, the Prince Fu.

FEI. Your slave, Yi Hsiang, the Prince Hui.

TSAI CHI. Your slave, Tsai Chi.

HSU TUNG. Your servant, Hsu Tung, the Grand Secretary.

TZU HSI [*raising her hand impatiently*]. Enough, now! We give you leave to dispense with the usual procedure.

114

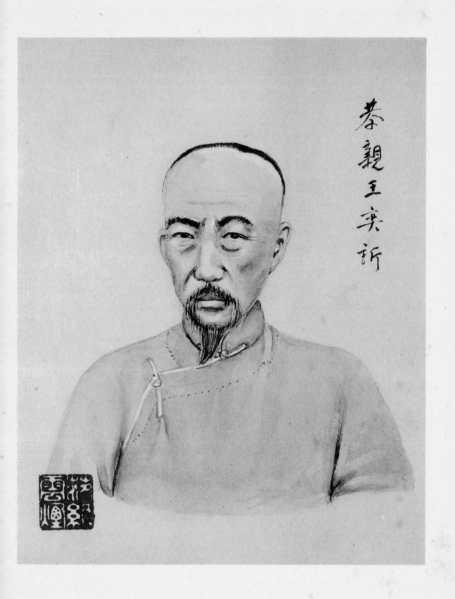

恭親王奕訢

PRINCE KUNG

(*A wizened little man with a wisp of a beard*)

[The rest take up their places in silence, while she proceeds to address them in her grand manner.]

We have news of the gravest import. His Majesty, as you will have heard, contracted smallpox some time ago. The disease ran its course and he appeared to be much better, when this evening he complained of giddiness, and before medical aid could be rendered, mounted the Dragon and ascended to Heaven. We were prostrated with grief . . .

[Tzu An breaks out in loud sobs.]

. . . but reflecting that Our private feelings must not be allowed to interfere with Our duties to the State . . .

[She looks sternly at Tzu An, who hurriedly wipes her tears.]

. . . We have summoned the Dynastic Council with a minimum of delay. His Majesty having passed away without issue and without nominating an Heir, the Council must now decide who is to succeed to the Throne.

Tzu An. I heard that A-Lu-Té is . . . is in the family way . . .

Tzu Hsi *[ignoring her]*. As there are troubles with the Mohammedans, with the French Barbarians and with the Japanese Dwarfs, the Throne must not be vacant for a single day. Now, the Council is well aware that His Highness, Yi Fan, the Prince Chun, has a son who is one of the possible heirs. As His Highness is Our sister's husband, and ill disposed persons might hereafter allege that We exerted pressure to obtain the nomination for Our nephew, We shall take no part in the discussion.

Kung. The Council much appreciates Your Majesty's disinterestedness. It may be stated, however, that only His Highness Tsai Chi's son, His Highness Pu Lun, conforms to the ritual requirement that he belong to a generation below the Emperor who has started the Grand Journey.

[Tsai Chi kow-tows and murmurs his gratitude.]

Tzu Hsi. True. But His Highness Tsai Chi's father was adopted by a distant branch. There are no precedents for bringing back someone, who has been adopted by other branches, to continue the Imperial line.

Jung Lu *[entering and kneeling]*. Your slave, Jung Lu, begs leave to make his report.

Tzu Hsi. Go on.

Jung Lu. The Imperial Guards at all the Gates of the Purple Forbidden City have been trebled. Without permission from Your Majesty, no person is allowed to pass.

TZU HSI. Good. [*to the Council*] A mere formality, gentlemen, against the possibility of disaffection either without—or within. [*to Jung Lu*] You may go.

[*Jung Lu goes out and there follows a hurried consultation in whispers among the members, who appear apprehensive.*]

TSAI CHI. As has been pointed out, there is a certain legal weakness in my son's case, and I hereby withdraw his candidature.

TZU HSI. Maybe it is prudent of you to do so, though We trust that in this decision you are guided wholly by the advice of your colleagues.

TSAI CHI. Entirely so, Your Majesty—that and, as you say, by prudence.

TZU AN. But how about Prince Kung's son? I like him best. He is such a dear boy, most kind to animals.

[*Prince Kung kow-tows but says nothing.*]

TUN. If primogeniture is to be observed, His Highness Prince Kung's son has the better claim, for His Highness Prince Chun is the younger brother.

TZU HSI. What have you to say, Prince Kung?

KUNG [*kow-towing*]. I am very grateful to Your Majesties . . .

JUNG LU [*entering and kneeling*]. Your slave, Jung Lu, begs leave to make his report.

TZU HSI. Yes?

JUNG LU. As an additional precaution I have caused a company of the Guard to surround this Hall.

TZU HSI. You have done well. [*to the Council*] These precautions should not alarm you, gentlemen, for We know you all to be loyal to the State. [*to Jung Lu*] You may go.

[*Jung Lu retires and the Council holds a further whispered consultation.*]

KUNG. The Council has decided to support the candidature of His Highness Prince Chun's son, Your Majesty's nephew. While giving due weight to the question of primogeniture, we think it is balanced by the great advantage which will accrue to the State from the accession of Prince Chun's son, for Your Majesty, whom we hereby request to undertake again the Regency with the Eastern Empress Dowager, will be well situated to give him every advice and instruction.

TZU AN [*dreamily*]. Goddess of Mercy! Have I to be Regent again?

KUNG. If Your Majesty pleases.

TZU AN. And who did you say is to be Emperor?

116

KUNG. Tsai Tien, Prince Chun's son, Your Majesty.

TZU AN. But he is a mere baby of three and a half years old.

TZU HSI. He'll be five next year, that is in twenty-five days.

TZU AN. But Prince Kung's boy is seventeen already!

KUNG. Even so, Your Majesty, we think our choice is a prudent one.

TZU HSI. Are We to take that as the vote of the Council?

KUNG. If Your Majesty pleases.

TZU HSI. Any one against?

[*There is a faint murmur. At that instant Jung Lu enters the room and kneels down as before.*]

JUNG LU. Your slave, Jung Lu, begs leave to make his report.

TZU HSI. One moment. [*to the Council*] Any one against?

KUNG [*hurriedly*]. The vote is unanimous, for I have already withdrawn my son's candidature.

ALL. The vote is unanimous!

TZU HSI. The Council, therefore, officially declares its unanimous support to the accession of His Highness Tsai Tien, eldest son of His Highness Prince Chun. . . .

[*Prince Chun knocks his head on the floor and breaks out in loud sobs.*]

CHUN. My poor son!

KUNG [*furiously*]. You fool, Yi Fan! [*to eunuchs*] Help His Highness out of the room.

TZU HSI. The Council is now adjourned. [*to Jung Lu*] Jung Lu, your presence is no longer required.

KUNG [*anxiously*]. May we have the necessary passes?

TZU HSI. Jung Lu, pass out all the members of the Council.

JUNG LU. Yes, Your Majesty.

[*Everybody heaves a sigh of relief and they file out, while Jung Lu lingers on.*]

TZU AN. Goddess of Mercy! I am so sleepy that I nearly fell off my chair. I'll be getting on, too. It's so late. And Dragon Eyes hates me leaving him at night. [*She goes.*]

TZU HSI. Jung Lu, you have served me well this evening. But we have not quite done. There is one more step. The new Emperor must be installed in the Palace to-night.

JUNG LU. It is nearly midnight, Your Majesty. It is snowing and bitterly cold. The child is delicate, they say.

TZU HSI. Ah, Jung Lu, you lack thoroughness. Attention to detail and speed are the keys of success. Take the Imperial Sedan and, with

117

a strong body of the Guard, go to Prince Chun's house at once and bring my sister and her son here.

JUNG LU. May I ask a favour, Your Majesty?

TZU HSI. I never refuse the requests of those who serve me well.

JUNG LU. His Highness the Prince Chun's second son, who is a year old, is not yet betrothed. My wife has just given me a humble daughter. May I beg . . . ?

TZU HSI. Well, Jung Lu, you are asking a very high price.

[*Jung Lu kneels and kow-tows.*]

However, I am prepared to pay it.

[*They all retire.*]

END OF SCENE THREE

[*Wen Li enters. The growing difficulty of his task has not lessened his assurance, probably because of the increased amount of stimulant he has taken. He says*]:

Boldness and decision, I know these appeal to you, but even so I feel that the elimination of a Son of Heaven may seem to require further justification. This I am happily able to give. You have been told, and have seen for yourselves, how the Almighty Mother's sole aim was the preservation of the State. To make this clearer and perhaps more convincing, it will be convenient to define what She meant by the word 'State'. Since coming to these Outer Regions my attention has been drawn to a parallel in their annals and to quote this will make my meaning plain. A one-time chieftain of the Red Barbarian tribe known as the French—his name being Louis No. 14, if I am properly informed—was in the habit of saying—to quote the jargon which passes for language in his country—'L'état c'est moi', the State, that is I. This was a literal translation of the Almighty Mother's phrase: 'Chen Chi Kuo Cha' or 'I am the State'. It follows therefore, that whatever appeared likely to hurt Her, would do the State harm and wherever She might expect advantage, there the State would also benefit. For a Barbarian chieftain like Louis No. 14 to make such a claim was laughable, for like all Barbarians he was without virtue. But for the Almighty Mother, it was a rightful claim.

In the next scene, which takes place seven years later, that is in the Seventh Year of the Reign of the Emperor Kuang Hsu—which, by the way, is the reign title of Prince Chun's son, the new Emperor —the Almighty Mother is obliged to perform a further painful duty, so that She, that is the State, may continue to flourish.

[*He bows, and, with a sad smile, retires.*]

SCENE IV

(The 11th of the 3rd Moon, the seventh year of the reign of Kuang Hsu, April 9th, 1881.)

The east part of the Palace of Tranquillity and Longevity in the Great Within is occupied by Her Majesty Tzu An, known for that reason as the Eastern Empress Dowager. As she is not an ostentatious person, her apartments are furnished in the simplest manner. The big and lofty chamber you see is used as her private living-room, leading, on one side, to her bedroom, and, on the other, to an ante-room. The time is about noon on a warm sunny day of spring. A large jade statue of the Goddess of Mercy stands in a shrine against the upper wall of the room.

Two eunuchs and two ladies-in-waiting enter and line up on two sides, to be followed immediately by Her Majesty the Eastern Empress Dowager. In her capacity as Regent, she has just concluded the morning audience. Now forty-five years old, she appears much older. Wearing her full court robes may give her dignity, but nevertheless they are such a heavy burden to her on a warm day that she looks more overwrought than usual.

TZU AN [*in a complaining voice*]. No matter how broad your shoulders may be, the heavy burden of the State will weigh them down.

[*She sinks into a comfortable chair in the middle of the room.*]
Court dress is even heavier than the burden of the State.

1ST LADY. May I help Your Majesty to change?

TZU AN. No, not yet. I'm expecting His Highness the Prince Kung, the Grand Adviser. Goddess of Mercy, I *am* hot!

2ND LADY. Your Majesty should not work so hard.

TZU AN. I've got to, and all by myself, till the Western Dowager is well again—that is, if she ever is!

1ST LADY. They say Her Majesty is much better to-day.

TZU AN. With all those horrible actors, painters and musicians round her, she will never be well again. She'll never be able to tear herself away from her . . . her . . . her favourite early enough to hold the morning audience. I'm ashamed of her. At her age, too!

2ND LADY [*who loves a bit of scandal*]. Be careful, Your Majesty, she may have spies here. But I heard that she was really in bed yesterday.

TZU AN. Yes, in bed yesterday and in bed to-day! Why, I called at her Palace after the Audience just now and that wretch, Li, tried to stop me by saying she was still in bed. But as I was half through the door, I saw . . . I . . . saw . . .

1ST LADY [*who loves a bit of scandal even more than the second lady*]. Oh, Your Majesty, do be careful! But what did you see?

2ND LADY [*desperately curious*]. Yes, what did you see?

TZU AN [*blushing, or perhaps red in the face with indignation*]. A pair of man's boots along with her shoes outside the curtain of her bed!

1ST AND 2ND LADIES [*smiling*]. Oh ! Oh!

TZU AN. And while she is indulging herself in such shameless ways, the full burden of the State falls on me. Oh, I miss A-Lu-Té, the Empress Chia Shun, terribly!

1ST LADY. She would have been a great help to Your Majesty at a time like this.

TZU AN. Yes, and though I know she was miserable, I think she might at least have considered me a little more before committing suicide. Grief for a husband is all very well, but it can be carried too far. And suicide by starvation—well, that wouldn't be my way of doing it! Which reminds me—I'm starved! What about lunch? I don't see it. It's late.

2ND LADY. Yes, Your Majesty, it's rather late to-day, and I've already despatched a eunuch to the Imperial Kitchen to inquire into the matter.

1ST LADY. In the meantime, would Your Majesty care for some cake to go on with?

TZU AN. I'd better not. It would only spoil my appetite. After having worked the whole morning, I don't want to spoil my lunch by having cake first.

2ND LADY. Since the morning audience takes such a long time, it might be a good idea to have a break in the middle for refreshments.

TZU AN. I quite agree with you, but the Grand Councillors would make difficulties if I proposed it. Unfortunately, I'm very much in their hands. For the first week after the Western Dowager gave up getting out of her bed in the morning, I found it very hard. She has a wonderful memory for precedents, I will say. But what precedent she has for keeping actors, painters and musicians in the Palace, I don't know! Anyhow, I now can have things my own way.

1ST LADY. And it must be rather nice for Your Majesty to have things your own way for a while.

Tzu An. Yes, I do enjoy that. And perhaps I'm not so stupid as some people make out. For instance, to-day [*lowering her voice*] I discovered a scandal, which has been going on for a long time, and evidently the all-knowing Western Dowager knows nothing about it yet!

[*Her suite move close to her, eager to listen.*]

2nd Lady. Another scandal, Your Majesty?

Tzu An. Not that sort. You remember all the talk about the navy, how the money was to be raised?

Ladies [*breathlessly*]. Yes, Your Majesty?

Tzu An. Well, there will be no navy!

Ladies. Why?

Tzu An. Because the money to build it—I forget exactly how much, for I'm not good at figures, but it was a lot—has been squandered instead on something else!

1st Lady. How disgraceful!

Tzu An. This came out in audience this morning because one of the Navy people memorialized. When I asked angrily for an explanation, Prince Kung, who as leader of the Council was kneeling nearest to me, whispered that he would bring me the documents after the audience. It would never do, he said, to explain in public. That's another reason why I'm in a hurry for my lunch.

2nd Lady. Shall we send a second eunuch to inquire?

Tzu An. I'd better wait. If we keep on sending, people will think me greedy.

[*A eunuch enters and kneels.*]

Eunuch. His Highness the Prince Kung is awaiting the sacred word.

Tzu An. I wish I could have my lunch first! But as there is no sign of it, I'll see him. Besides, it's urgent. Show His Highness in.

Eunuch [*going*]. Yes, Your Majesty.

Tzu An. Where is my Dragon Eyes? His Highness the Prince Kung always reminds me of my Dragon Eyes.

1st Lady. The maids have taken him out for a run in the garden.

2nd Lady. But why is it that His Highness reminds Your Majesty of the dog?

Tzu An. Because his son is so fond of my Dragon Eyes. I used to want him to be Emperor, but now Kuang Hsu has got so attached to me that I'm glad after all it was he who was selected. Call the maids in. I wish to see my Dragon Eyes.

122

1ST LADY. Yes, Your Majesty.

[*She sends a eunuch out to bring the dog in. In the meantime, His Highness Prince Kung enters. He is still wearing his court dress and has a small red lacquered leather despatch box under his arm. He starts to kneel but Tzu An stops him.*]

TZU AN. Get up, Your Highness. This is an informal occasion. Take a seat.

KUNG. Thank you, Your Majesty. [*He takes a seat at some distance from her.*] It will be understood that if Your Majesty had not demanded an explanation, your slave would never have ventured to bring up the matter.

TZU AN [*puzzled*]. Why, Your Highness? Why all this mystery? I intended to ask you more at the audience, but you whispered to me to wait until I'd seen you privately.

KUNG. If the matter were not highly confidential and urgent, I should not dare to intrude into your Majesty's private apartments, and at such an inconvenient time.

TZU AN. It fits in all right because I'm waiting for lunch.

KUNG. I shall not detain your Majesty many minutes. Before I begin, however, may I inquire whether Your Majesty's attendants are all trustworthy? On my way in, I thought I saw one of the Western Dowager's eunuchs leaving here.

TZU AN [*rather flustered*]. Of course everyone here is entirely trustworthy.

KUNG. I held it my duty to raise the point, and when Your Majesty hears the names of those involved, the reason will be clear.

TZU AN. Who are they?

KUNG [*dramatically*]. The Chief Eunuch and the Captain of the Imperial Guard!

TZU AN. Goddess of Mercy! Li Lien-Ying and Jung Lu!

KUNG. No less, Your Majesty.

TZU AN. Goddess of Mercy! Are you quite certain?

KUNG [*showing the box*]. The proofs are here.

TZU AN. Goddess of Mercy! How did it happen?

KUNG [*opening the box with a key and displaying various documents*]. I will leave these for Your Majesty to peruse at leisure. The facts, however, can be shortly stated. Li and Jung by bribes and threats suborned the officials of the Board of War to transfer the naval grant to the Board of Works. The sum was then given out to contractors for a new Summer Palace to be built near the one burnt by

123

Barbarians, ten per cent of the total sticking to the hands of Li and Jung.

Tzu An. Ten per cent? How much is a per cent?

Kung [*solemnly*]. They got several millions.

Tzu An. Goddess of Mercy! Several millions?

Kung. That may be an understatement. Not only has there been peculation on a grand scale, but, since the warships have not been built, the safety of the country has been put in jeopardy.

Tzu An [*standing up in great indignation*]. This is an outrage! But why didn't you tell us about it when you first got to know it? We must punish them severely.

Kung [*kneeling*]. Your slave craves Your Majesty's pardon, but he was waiting for a suitable opportunity. Your Majesty will understand—

Tzu An. I understand it is the duty of every one of us to discover such treacherous acts and bring the traitors to justice. I know I am not a very capable and experienced person like the Western Dowager. . . .

Kung [*hurriedly*]. Your Majesty underestimates very much your capacity and experience. Counting the two Regencies together, Your Majesty has ruled the State for some twenty years. No doubt during that time the Western Dowager has sat as co-Regent, but we members of the Grand Council have learned to respect Your Majesty's judgment and rectitude, and in the present crisis—for so serious a case of maladministration can only be called a crisis—we know where to look for a lead.

Tzu An [*very much flattered*]. Get up and sit down, Your Highness. I have certainly tried my best. The Western Dowager . . .

[*She begins to reflect a little while Prince Kung resumes his seat.*]

Now that we mention the Western Dowager, I wonder whether . . . I wonder whether . . . Oh, Goddess of Mercy! I am sure I am in a mess now!

Kung [*craftily*]. Your Majesty will please rest assured that while the Western Dowager has her supporters and admirers, her recent behaviour, both public and private, has made her the laughing stock of the whole Empire. Your Majesty has only to give the order, and the whole Court will do your bidding as one man!

Tzu An [*waveringly*]. There's no possibility, I hope, no, I pray, of her having been in any way what you might call mixed up in this affair? It didn't strike me till this minute, but suppose it turned out she were—Goddess of Mercy! she would never forgive me if I took any action against Li and Jung.

KUNG. Since Your Majesty has brought the matter up, it is necessary to be very firm. Among these documents Your Majesty will find three strongly worded remonstrances by Imperial Censors. I kept them back simply because I desired to wait for an opportunity like the present one, when Your Majesty would be well placed to take action. [*very solemnly*] Our descendants will forever remember what a great Empress Your Majesty was.

TZU AN [*quite undecided*]. Of course I want to do my duty. But . . . but . . . but both Li and Jung are more than the Western Dowager's trusted subordinates. Why, they are her favourites. And talking of her favourites, I went to try to see her and tell her about this scandal, and what do you think I saw in her private apartments?

KUNG. I dare not guess, Your Majesty.

TZU AN. You are right. A pair of men's boots! And the horrid Li hustled me out!

KUNG. Then the path to take will be clear to Your Majesty. The choice is between the contempt and the admiration of posterity. Can Your Majesty hesitate? No. The chance is now or never. For the Western Dowager is not a woman to be trifled with. Once she guessed you had found her out—well, you know what would happen then!

TZU AN. Goddess of Mercy! Indeed, I do! But what do you want? You haven't said yet.

KUNG. In a matter of this kind speed is essential, and I submit that in audience to-morrow morning Your Majesty cause to be read an indictment against Li and Jung, when they may be arrested and handed over to the Board of Punishments. If Your Majesty consents, I will have it prepared. We look to Your Majesty to see justice done. If Your Majesty fails us, to whom can we turn?

TZU AN [*carried away by the animation of feeling important for the first time in her life*]. You may prepare the—what did you call it?—the indictment?

KUNG. Yes, Your Majesty, the indictment. I knew Your Majesty would act in a way 'proper, great, bright and illustrious', as is written on the board hanging on the middle beam of the Main Palace. Your Majesty's tenure of the Regency will be a memorable epoch in the dynastic history.

[*He hands her the box, bows and leaves. As the ladies gaze at her, she, in high spirits, passes the box to them.*]

TZU AN. And now for lunch! Go and bring it in this instant! I'll look into these papers immediately afterwards.

[*Another eunuch enters the room and kneels.*]

EUNUCH. The Imperial cook craves Your Majesty's pardon for the delay in the Imperial Luncheon. He explains that a certain eunuch, who was intoxicated, picked a quarrel with the Master of the Dishes, and smashed up all the Imperial victuals already prepared. A second lunch is now under speedy preparation and will be served to Your Majesty in the course of the next hour.

TZU AN [*really angry*]. Goddess of Mercy! In the course of the next hour! I am famishing! I'm already famished! Send the cook to me! Send the drunken eunuch to me!

EUNUCH. Yes, Your Majesty.

[*As this eunuch goes out, a second eunuch enters and kneels.*]

2ND EUNUCH. Her Majesty the Western Dowager has sent Your Majesty some Mongolian cakes.

[*A eunuch from the Western Dowager enters, holding a trayful of fancy cakes. He kneels in front of Tzu An.*]

W. EUNUCH. As the Imperial luncheon is delayed, the Western Dowager sends these Mongolian dainties, which she has just received and tasted and found delicious. She hopes that Your Majesty will sample a few while you are waiting.

TZU AN [*thankfully*]. How very thoughtful of her. They look heavenly.

[*Dragon Eyes is now brought in by a maid and he jumps into Tzu An's lap. But she takes no notice of him for her eyes are fixed on the cakes.*]

W. EUNUCH. Yes, Your Majesty. So the Western Dowager said.

[*He holds up the tray and offers the cakes to Tzu An, who, with beaming face, takes one and stuffs it whole into her mouth. They are of rather small size.*]

TZU AN. That's good! [*taking another*] Light as a feather! [*taking a third*] They are appetizers, really. [*taking a fourth*] You might eat a dozen of them without spoiling [*taking a fifth*] your appetite in the least. [*taking two more*] It was indeed very thoughtful of the Western Dowager [*swallowing with satisfaction*]. She is a good woman. [*to eunuch*] Thank her, will you.

W. EUNUCH. Yes, Your Majesty.

TZU AN. You can go now, but leave the tray. [*looking at the three remaining cakes*] Wait! [*taking one, swallowing it in a hurry and picking up the other two*] Now you may take it. And don't forget the message.

W. EUNUCH [*going*]. No, Your Majesty.

TZU AN [*contentedly*]. I feel more myself. [*noticing her dog for the*

126

first time]. Oh, my poor Dragon Eyes! I'd forgotten all about you. Would you like to share these two cakes with your Empress. Here, have this one [*putting it in front of him*] But you shan't have them both, greedy! [*eating the other cake*] Don't you like it?

[*The dog will not touch the cake. She pushes it closer and he turns further away.*]

You silly dog, it's delicious!

[*The sun goes in, and it becomes less bright in the room. Tzu An looks round.*]

Is there going to be a shower?

1ST LADY. It looks like thunder.

[*Tzu An tries the cake on the dog again, and once more he turns away from it.*]

TZU AN. This is the last time. If you refuse it, I'll have it myself.

[*The dog remains obstinate. She takes the cake back.*]

Now look!

[*She opens her mouth wide and is about to stuff the last cake into it, when a spasm passes over her face and she stops abruptly.*]

I feel a bit shivery.

2ND LADY. Are you sure, Your Majesty? It seems very close.

TZU AN. Hasn't it got cooler?

[*It grows a little darker.*]

1ST LADY. I believe there *is* going to be a thunderstorm.

[*Tzu An is not listening. She looks at the cake and then lets it drop from her hand. She tries to pick it up, but when she stretches her hand down she lurches and nearly falls from her chair.*]

2ND LADY [*alarmed*]. Is Your Majesty unwell?

TZU AN [*breathlessly*]. I felt a sudden sharp pain, but it passed.

[*Another spasm shakes her. She drops the dog.*]

Oh, Goddess of Mercy!

1ST LADY [*startled*]. Your Majesty is not well!

TZU AN [*faintly*]. I don't know what's happened. Let me lie down.

[*Before her ladies can catch her, she falls from her chair. They rush forward and carry her to a couch. The room is now almost dark. Several eunuchs enter and remain watching in the shadows by the door.*]

I feel easier now. Let me rest.

[*As she speaks she is seized by a more violent spasm.*]

2ND LADY. We must get Her Majesty into bed.

1ST LADY. Send for the Grand Physician, quick!

[*The ladies carry Tzu An into the inner room and the dog follows them in.*]

127

A eunuch runs for the Physician, but he finds the door is barred by other eunuchs.]

EUNUCH. Oh!

[*He is greatly alarmed when he sees Li Lien-Ying coming into the room from behind these eunuchs.*]

LI [*quite at his ease*]. The whole court of the Eastern Empress Dowager is to be placed under arrest, each person to be confined separately until further orders. [*Pointing to Tzu An's eunuch*] Seize that fellow first.

[*His minions obey and then scatter in all directions. Two go into the inner room and conduct out the ladies-in-waiting, amid the loud barks of the dog. Li now goes towards the comfortable chair and sits down. There are still three or four eunuchs attending on him. Jung Lu, in his uniform and with a sapphire button, enters. Li greets him casually.*]

JUNG LU. Is she dead?

LI. It won't be long now. Half one of those cakes was enough to kill a giant in a quarter of an hour, and the greedy old thing swallowed the whole lot except one! She should be stone dead any moment. But have you secured Prince Kung?

JUNG LU. He was detained as he was about to leave the Meridian Gate.

LI. He will get no mercy. Further information has just come in that he intended to sweep away the whole régime. After he had arrested us, he plotted to seize the Palace, retire the Holy Mother and place his own brat on the Dragon Throne, with himself as Regent.

JUNG LU. Did the Eastern Dowager guess what was in the wind?

LI [*laughing heartily*]. Good Heavens, no!

JUNG LU. Anyhow, she deserved her fate. She was an idiot of a woman. Are your people in position?

LI. A rat could not escape them. And your men are at their posts, I suppose?

JUNG LU. An iron hoop has been cast around the city.

IMPERIAL EMISSARY [*entering the room in court dress and standing in the centre*]. I am the bearer of an Imperial Mandate.

[*All kneel while he reads.*]

'The sudden demise of the Empress Dowager Tzu An, has been reported . . . '

LI [*looking up*]. Stop a moment, please. What do you mean exactly by the word 'demise'?

李蓮英肖像

LI LIEN-YING

(Crafty, cold, hard and insolent)

EMISSARY [*blandly*]. I haven't the faintest idea.

JUNG LU. It's a grand way of saying 'gone west'.

LI [*getting to his feet*]. I thought so. But the old girl may not be quite dead yet. You there, hold on for a second until I make sure.

[*Rolling up his sleeves calmly, he goes into the inner room. The fierce barking of the dog is heard and then a crash, and the dog's faint moans. There follows a distant clap of thunder and soon Li's voice is heard from within.*]

All right now. Go ahead.

[*While the Emissary resumes his reading, Li comes out and, coolly turning down his sleeves, kneels at his original place.*]

EMISSARY. 'The sudden demise of the Empress Dowager, Tzu An, has been reported and We desire to place on record at once the profound grief into which this intelligence has plunged Us. Her Majesty has been Our colleague for twenty years and her counsel was always highly valued. That she should now fall a victim to a fatal disease is a sad and irreparable loss. As the disease which so suddenly carried her away has, We are informed, a malignant character, We direct that no person, whether related to her or not, be permitted to view her body, which shall be enclosed forthwith in a coffin and nailed down. Respect this!' A Myriad Years!

ALL [*kow-towing*]. A Myriad Years!

[*The Imperial Emissary departs to read the Mandate in the various palaces of the Forbidden City. The others rise to their feet.*]

LI [*wistfully*]. The Holy Mother has a wonderful turn of phrase.

JUNG LU. And also a wonderful head for detail.

LI [*with genuine admiration in his voice*]. Yes, everything has been thought of, everything arranged so well. What a marvellous feeling for propriety she has! And all done at such short notice! Well, we had better go and see about the coffin.

[*The sun is now shining again and the room is bright. As they leave the place a number of kitchen eunuchs, preceded by a butler eunuch, enter, bearing trays with steaming dishes.*]

BUTLER EUNUCH. The Imperial Luncheon!

[*Seeing nobody is in the room, they turn back without putting down the trays.*]

END OF SCENE FOUR

END OF ACT TWO

129   I

[*Wen Li enters with a smile and says*]:

During the interval, which I trust has been spent by all of you, not in emptying wine-cups or patting sing-song girls, but in virtuous conversation or in reciting the Classics, the unworthy person who is addressing you withdrew to a private apartment and there reviewed —as he has so often done with profit—the history of the Holy Mother, recalling in succession Her happy adolescence, Her fortunate entry into the Palace, the period of Her co-regency and lastly of Her sole regency.

For a number of years, as you will be shown in this Third Act, She continued alone to guide the Celestial Empire, though often attempting to seek a dignified retirement in the New Summer Palace, built to replace that feloniously burnt by the Red Barbarians. But whenever She sought release from Her high duties and in the peace of Her lovely retreat had begun to practise calligraphy or study the Odes, circumstances obliged Her to return to the Dragon Seat. We shall sympathize with Her and wish that She had been blessed, as She deserved, with more worthy descendants, to whom She might confidently have delegated Her authority.

We begin this act in the twentieth year of the Reign of Kuang Hsu, that is, the year 1894 according to your nonsensical and un-authorized calendar. It seems only the other day to me. The Great Mother is sixty years of age and Her nephew, the Emperor Kuang Hsu, is twenty-four. Six years previously She had handed over to him the power of the State, after marrying him to his cousin and her niece. The young Empress Lung Yu, to call her by her title, is also a Ye-ho-na-la, for she is none other than the daughter of the Holy Mother's noble brother, His Grace the Duke Kwei Hsiang, about whom Her Majesty has desired me to withhold all information.

When you are allowed to gaze on Her again, you will see Her, elderly and sublime, celebrating Her sixtieth birthday by a picnic on the Marble Barge at the Summer Palace. Earlier in the year the barbarous Dwarfs of Japan had had the effrontery to send their troops and ships against the Imperial forces, but the Great Mother rightly judged that war should not be allowed to interfere with the proper observance of so propitious an occasion.

[*He bows and retires.*]

ACT III
SUPREMACY
SCENE I

(The 10th of the 10th Moon, the twentieth year of the reign of Kuang Hsu, November 7th, 1894.)

If the Old Summer Palace of the Round Bright Garden was considered the most beautiful retreat in China, the New Summer Palace of the All-Nourishing Harmonious Park is ten thousand ten times more beautiful. With the All-Bright Lake in front and the Mountain of Ten Thousand Years behind, the place sings aloud of paradise. Its construction was carried out on an elaborate plan, and no expense was spared. The very best building material was collected from every part of the Empire and hundreds of skilled workmen have been busy over it for years. If those who have criticized the Empress Dowager for squandering on a private pleasure garden the money which ought to have been used to build a navy for the nation, could be invited to look at it, their acrimony would certainly be softened with admiration.

Here in the garden you see a choice landscape of strongly contrasted and bright colours. The buildings are lacquered red, with roofs of green, yellow and dark blue tiles. Some trees are evergreens, and here and there the frost has tinted their leaves with gold. In the midst of all this rich profusion, perhaps the most beautiful corner is the shore of the All-Bright Lake, where stands the Marble Barge.

This is a pavilion built of white carved marble in the form of a pleasure boat. Standing as if moored to the lakeside, its double shimmers in the placid water, under a firmament flecked with autumn clouds.

A procession enters and approaches the Barge. At the head of it in sedan chairs are the Dowager Empress Tzu Hsi and her niece, the Empress Lung Yu, both dressed in embroidered satin gowns and black satin hats decorated with fresh chrysanthemums. Walking behind are Ladies-in-Waiting, the Chief Eunuch, Li Lien-Ying, and attendant eunuchs, together with a number of Court artists, musicians and others. At the rear are maids and servant-eunuchs, carrying picnic baskets and other appointments.

As Tzu Hsi alights from her sedan, the Empress Lung Yu, who

has vacated hers a moment earlier, hurries forward to help the Dowager. It must be noted here that while Tzu Hsi is, as she always has been, either in her movements or at rest, either in her speeches or when silent, every inch an Empress, Her Majesty the Empress Lung Yu, in spite of her title and though a pretty woman in her early twenties, looks no more than a well-trained maid. Even if her appearance had been dignified she would have been hard put to it to seem so with her aunt ordering her about and continually finding fault.

We are told that Tzu Hsi is now sixty and that she is elderly and sublime. Sublime, yes; elderly, by no means. If she is sixty, she should be elderly, but she does not look a day more than thirty-nine. This may seem impossible. But the beauty-culture department of the Palace possessed secrets which the parlours of the West have still to learn. Tzu Hsi was probably the best turned out woman the world has ever seen.

Tzu Hsi. When one is busy, the days fly fast. But I have been retired from the helm of State for six years, and feel years have flown even faster than days.

[*She turns and looks at the Marble Barge.*]

How lovely the Marble Barge looks this morning with its reflection in the lake! It was thus I imagined it when I was designing the Park. No previous Sovereign has had a marble pavilion that seemed to float. Our great ancestors, Kang Hsi and Chien Lung, had some pretty fancies at the Round Bright Garden, but—and I speak with every respect—nothing they built can compare with this. [*sharply to the Empress*] Do you not agree with me, Empress?

Lung Yu. Alas! Old Ancestor, the treasures at Yuan-Ming-Yuan were burnt before I was born.

Tzu Hsi [*rather piqued*]. That may be so, but have you not heard from those who saw them?

Lung Yu [*hurriedly*]. Indeed, yes! Everyone says that the new Palaces erected by the Old Ancestor are in every way superior.

Tzu Hsi [*disagreeably*]. I am too old to care for compliments, but in this case it is the bare truth. Look at the Marble Barge—I repeat, it seems to float.

Lung Yu [*meekly*]. Yes, Old Ancestor, it floats, indeed.

Tzu Hsi [*entering the barge*]. Why don't you go and see about the refreshments? What are you standing here for?

隆裕太后

EMPRESS LUNG YU

(No more than a well-trained maid)

LUNG YU [moving immediately]. With your permission, Old Ancestor.

TZU HSI [looking about]. Where are my cushions?

LI [hurries forward with cushions]. Here they are, Old Ancestor.

[He is greatly aged. When he was young, he seemed to be tall, handsome and smart, but now he is stout and ugly, and his gait, though still firm, has slowed down. He goes to the forepart of the barge, where stands the Chair of State, and places the cushions on it. With haughty steps, Tzu Hsi walks to her Chair and sits down. Her ladies follow, to stand right and left behind her. Then Li beckons to the Court artists.]

Come, hurry up and take your places at the stern!

[The artists file on to the Barge. Li signals to the musicians, who remain on shore.]

Get ready and wait for the Sacred Word.

[The Empress is moving about, busying herself with the arrangements. Tzu Hsi surveys her activities and is not satisfied.]

TZU HSI. Hey! Empress, why are you having that table put there?

LUNG YU. I thought we could use it as a side table. . .

TZU HSI [grudgingly]. Very well. Get your table ready first! But where is my table?

LUNG YU [signalling to the servants to bring it and place it in front of the Dowager]. They couldn't bring the table before the Old Ancestor had taken her seat.

TZU HSI. Don't answer me back! I do not want your excuses. [frowning upon seeing her table] This table will never do. It ought to be of red lacquer.

LUNG YU [looking about]. They do not seem to have brought a red lacquer table. The Old Ancestor liked this table yesterday. . . .

TZU HSI [angrily]. But yesterday I was dressed in black! You should have a little more common sense, Empress. This one will not do, I say. Remove it at once! It clashes with my dress. What sort of picture will my artists paint if the colours are wrong?

LUNG YU [to a eunuch]. Go and bring a red lacquer table quickly.

TZU HSI [capriciously, as another eunuch begins to remove the offending table]. No, leave it where it is. We cannot start sending for another table now. [to Empress] You should have seen to that before. What a pity your taste is so deplorable!

LUNG YU [moving to see about the dishes and wines]. Yes, Old Ancestor.

TZU HSI [to the artists, who have taken their position at a long table in the stern, facing her]. Are you ready? Why don't you start now? What are you waiting for?

133

CHIEF ARTIST [*signals to rest to begin*]. Yes, Holy Mother.

TZU HSI. The title of the picture to-day is 'Her Majesty on Her Sixtieth Birthday Surrounded by Her Family'. [*looking round her*] I don't see a single member of my family round me! Empress, where are you?

LUNG YU [*running to her from the shore*]. Coming, Old Ancestor. I didn't know you wanted me here. I was looking after the wines.

TZU HSI. Excuses, excuses! I don't want them. You stand here below on my right, and my niece-in-law, the Princess Chun—where is she, where is she?

[*Her Highness the Princess Chun is that daughter of Jung Lu whom we have seen betrothed in infancy to Prince Chun's second son, the brother of the Emperor. She is now twenty years of age. Being gaily dressed, profusely powdered and rouged, and very young, it is impossible to determine whether she is pretty or not. But she has very pretty movements and manners, perhaps a little too pretty for a lady of quality. She has been standing at the extreme end of the bow and looking at the distant scenery. Now she hurries to Tzu Hsi's side with a coquettish smile.*]

PRINCESS. Here I am, Old Ancestor.

TZU HSI [*evidently this is her favourite*]. Ah, you are the only one who cares what happens to me. Stand here, next to the Empress. Make a little room for her, Empress. Now, as soon as the Emperor comes, he will take this chair on my left. Meanwhile somebody had better sit for him. [*to Li, who is standing behind her*] Li, get a young eunuch to sit for the Emperor till he arrives.

LI. Yes, Old Ancestor.

[*He signals to a good-looking young eunuch, who comes forward towards Tzu Hsi.*]

Hey, you come!

TZU HSI. No, he is too handsome, Li. See the way he holds himself. I want somebody like the Emperor, a miserable-looking object.

LI [*demurely*]. The Old Ancestor deigns to joke.

[*He signals to another eunuch, who looks like a nervous wreck, to come forward.*]

TZU HSI. No, I'm quite serious. This one is better, but still not quite wretched enough. However, he'll do. The fact is, Li, the Emperor's appearance is not his strong point, though if you ask what his strong point is, I'm afraid I can't tell you!

LI [*in a privileged aside*]. His strong point is his obedience to the Old Ancestor's commands.

Tzu Hsi [*pretending not to hear and looking towards the artists*]. Have you started?

CHIEF ARTIST. Yes, Holy Mother.

Tzu Hsi [*looking about her*]. Where are the Imperial Concubines, Pearl and Jade?

[*Her Highness, the Imperial Concubine Jade, an attractive girl of nineteen but with a depressed expression, comes forward from behind Tzu Hsi.*]

JADE. Your slave maid, Jade, is here, Old Ancestor, behind you all the time.

Tzu Hsi [*frowning*]. I knew you were there! But let me see you from time to time. Now, stand next to the Emperor's chair so that you will be in the picture. But where is your sister, the Pearl Concubine?

LUNG YU. She asked the Old Ancestor's pardon in case she were late and . . .

Tzu Hsi [*curtly*]. She is already very late! What is detaining her? It is her duty to be present in my birthday picture.

LUNG YU. Her intention was to join the procession, but at the last moment she received a message from the Emperor. It seemed that some important despatches had arrived . . .

Tzu Hsi [*her face bleak with rage*]. Despatches! What has a concubine to do with despatches! [*catching sight of the artists at work and forcing a smile*] I hope you were not drawing my face just then. Remember, I'm to look Motherly and Auspicious.

[*She adopts a motherly and auspicious expression.*]

CHIEF ARTIST. The Holy Mother's face is always divine.

Tzu Hsi. I daresay, but to-day I want to be painted looking happy at the head of my family, my happy family.

[*She looks at her happy family. The Empress is making a wry face as she tries to smile at her. The Princess is bored and watching the clouds. The Imperial Concubine Jade is knitting her eyebrows and looking at her own nose. The eunuch who is posing as the Emperor is sunk in a sort of nervous torpor. She is furious.*]

Good Heavens! You all look as if you were attending my funeral!

[*They all smile.*]

Ah! That makes you smile, to hear of my funeral! But I am still good for a few years more!

LI [*trying to smooth over matters*]. May I order the musicians to start, Old Ancestor?

Tzu Hsi. Yes, and have wine and refreshments served now.

[*Li signals to the musicians, who immediately start to play some soft music.*]

135

He also beckons the eunuchs to bring up the trays of dishes, a wine pot and a cup, and they are placed on the table before Tzu Hsi. Just then the Imperial Concubine Pearl appears on the bank in her sedan. She alights from it and, accompanied by two maids, steps on to the Barge and when at a respectful distance from Tzu Hsi kneels and kow-tows.

The Imperial Concubine Pearl is an extremely beautiful girl of twenty. She is dressed in exquisite taste and seems to be more self-possessed than anybody else. However, Tzu Hsi receives her obeisance icily. Putting her cup down with a frown, she looks away from the Concubine.]

PEARL. Your slave girl, the Concubine Pearl, begs to . . .

TZU HSI [*cutting in*]. You are very late! What have you been doing?

[*Pearl is silent; Tzu Hsi's annoyance increases.*]

I know what you have been doing. Presuming on the notice that the fool of an Emperor has taken of you, you have been putting forward your advice on affairs of State. Let me warn you of the dangers you run. The Emperor has his Ministers to advise him on matters of routine administration, and all important questions are referred to me. There is no room whatever for interference by a concubine. Anything done behind my back is conspiracy. Do you know the fate that awaits conspirators?

[*Her glance happens to alight on the artists. She forces a smile and adopts her motherly and auspicious expression once more.*]

Now get up and take your place beside your sister. The Court artists are doing a portrait of the happy family. How can I be happy with people like you annoying me!

PEARL [*getting up and going to her sister*]. Thank you, Old Ancestor.

[*At this moment the Emperor Kuang Hsu's yellow sedan approaches the bank. It is accompanied by a small company of the Imperial Guard and a number of eunuchs. They stop at a little distance from the lake and he alights and walks dejectedly towards the Barge. He is twenty-four years old but looks much older, is of medium stature and slightly bent. Tzu Hsi was speaking the truth when she said that there was a miserable air about him. Were he not wearing his Emperor's dress and coral button, he would look no better than the nervous eunuch who is sitting for him. He has a very soft voice and, whenever sternly questioned by his aunt, he is liable to mutter inaudibly or even to stutter. But normally he is quite articulate, though he seldom speaks above a whisper. Leaving his followers on shore, he enters the Barge and advances towards Tzu Hsi. On reaching the foot of her dais he kneels and kow-tows, murmuring his respects to her. She speaks sharply to him.*]

EMPEROR KUANG HSU

(. . . *a miserable air about him*)

Tzu Hsi. All right, all right! Get up at once and take the place of the eunuch here on my left. You are late.

Kuang Hsu [*scarcely audible*]. I have bad news to report . . .

Tzu Hsi [*angrily*]. Get up, when I tell you! I can't hear your murmurings.

Kuang Hsu [*still kneeling, but speaking louder*]. I have b-bad . . .

Tzu Hsi [*impatiently*]. Bad what? Bad manners? I know you have.

Kuang Hsu [*with some effort*]. I have b-bad news . . .

Tzu Hsi. Bad news! Well, I don't want to hear it on my birthday. Now get up and sit where I told you to. And for Heaven's sake smile and look cheerful for once in your life.

[*Kuang Hsu steals a glance at Pearl, as if for guidance or encouragement. She makes a hardly perceptible sign. He tries again to explain to the Dowager. But he is much shaken and almost unable to express himself.*]

Kuang Hsu. I am a-a-afraid that the . . .

Tzu Hsi. What?

Kuang Hsu. The Jap . . . ap . . . the Jap . . . ap . . .

Tzu Hsi [*jocularly*]. Oh, the Jap-ap, is it? And how are the Jap-aps?

[*There is general laughter.*]

Good! [*to the artists*] If we could induce the Emperor to tell us a story, you'd get a very good portrait of the happy family.

Kuang Hsu [*taking out some papers nervously from his sleeve and opening them in a pitiful way*]. If Your Majesty will read for yourself, you . . .

Tzu Hsi. What do you say? I can't hear.

Kuang Hsu [*pointing to a place in a paper*]. This little . . . just this little b-bit . . .

Tzu Hsi. I'm not going to read any document now. This is a picnic and we are having our portraits painted. Sit where I've told you. [*calling*] Li, assist the Emperor to rise and conduct him to his chair.

Li. Yes, Old Ancestor.

[*Li goes to the Emperor and pulls him none too gently to his feet.*]

Kuang Hsu. But we mu-mu-must . . .

Tzu Hsi. Yes, we must go on with the picnic.

Kuang Hsu [*glancing nervously at Pearl and receiving from her further encouraging signs*] . . . re-reinforce our troops im-immediately.

Tzu Hsi. Stop talking, Emperor. I'm not holding a war council now. All necessary measures for driving away the Japanese Dwarfs have been taken by me and we need not go into them to-day.

[*Li pushes the Emperor into the chair.*]

137

Now, Li, tell the musicians to play the tune 'The Triumphant Return of the Imperial Army'.

LI. Yes, Old Ancestor.

[*He jerks his head at one of the eunuchs who hurries on shore to give this instruction to the musicians. Immediately they start a loud tune, which lasts for some time, when a man is seen running towards the Marble Barge. He is dressed in the livery of a messenger of the Grand Council and he shouts loudly from the bank.*]

MESSENGER. I have an urgent message from the Board of War.

[*As he is not heard above the music he shouts louder.*]

An urgent message from the Board of War!

[*The music stops and Tzu Hsi darts a baleful look at the messenger and then turns to Li.*]

TZU HSI. Li, tell him to enter and not dare to shout again.

LI. Yes, Old Ancestor.

[*Li jerks his head and a eunuch goes on shore to conduct the messenger on board. He kneels at a distance from their Majesties.*]

TZU HSI. What is your message?

MESSENGER. Admiral Ting's fleet has been sunk by the Japanese Dwarfs.

[*There is a long pause of consternation. Tzu Hsi's fierce eye transfixes the Emperor, who seems to say, 'You see, I told you so.' She is further enraged and shouts at him in a terrible voice.*]

TZU HSI. Draw up an order for Admiral Ting's immediate dismissal and arrest!

[*Pearl makes a sign to the Emperor who gets up from his chair and kneels before Tzu Hsi.*]

KUANG HSU. Admiral Ting is a brave man . . .

TZU HSI. What? Speak up, can't you!

KUANG HSU. I say he is a b-b-brave man, it was not his f-fault. He hadn't en-enough sh-ships . . .

TZU HSI. Not his fault! Why not? He was in command of the fleet! If he had not enough ships, he should have asked for more.

KUANG HSU. He d-did. That was what I was trying to re-report, but Your Ma-Majesty would not l-listen.

TZU HSI. How could I tell what you were stammering about? In any case, it was too late to reinforce him.

KUANG HSU. But he complained b-before. He couldn't get sh-ships, because Your Ma . . . because the m-money . . . because the s-s-Summer Palace . . .

138

TZU HSI [*exceedingly angry*]. The Summer Palace! How dare you!
What do you understand of high policy? The face which the Dynasty
lost through the Red Barbarians burning the Old Palace could only
be recovered by building a new and better one. That recovery was
worth a thousand ships and thanks to me it was achieved. And yet
you have the impertinence to hint I did wrong in building this
Palace! Besides, Admiral Ting's defeat had nothing to do with the
Palace. It was due to his neglect to train his men. Have you ever
thought why I had this lake dug? For the training of the sailors, of
course, and it was dug here so that I could conveniently oversee the
training. But did Admiral Ting ever exercise his men on it? Not
that I know of! Drink was his only exercise, and women!

[*She raises her hand as if lifting a wine cup to her mouth and superbly
mimics a stout man patting a sing-song girl. The Emperor is silenced and
dare not even look towards Pearl. He continues to kneel, with an abject
expression on his face.*]

Such an Admiral is a disgrace to the Empire. He shall be brought
to the Capital for condign punishment. Issue an Imperial Edict for
his arrest at once.

KUANG HSU [*meekly*]. Yes, Your Ma-Majesty!

[*While he is creeping back to his seat, a second messenger is seen running
towards the Marble Barge. As he approaches, he shouts loudly.*]

2ND MESSENGER. An urgent message! An urgent message from the
Board of War!

TZU HSI [*to Li*]. Stop that lunatic, Li. I'm tired of hearing of
Admiral Ting's defeat!

[*Li sends a eunuch to prevent the messenger from coming on to the Barge.
But the man kneels on the bank and shouts.*]

2ND MESSENGER. I am charged to inform Your Majesty that
Admiral Ting, after memorializing the Throne, has committed
suicide!

TZU HSI [*to the Emperor, fiercely, after a pause*]. Issue an Imperial
Edict for his posthumous dismemberment!

[*She stands up and looks at the Court in general.*]

I had hoped in old age to enjoy some leisure, to paint and read and
visit my gardens, but even from a picnic I am called back to my desk.
[*to the Empress*] Cancel the festivities and tell the maids and eunuchs
to pack up. I will return at once. [*to Li*] No rewards for the musicians
to-day, and tell the artists to bring up their pictures.

[*Li directs a eunuch to tell the musicians the bad news, and signals to the artists to approach with their work. The artists do so, kneeling before the dais and each holding out his picture. Li collects them and hands them to Tzu Hsi, who scans them and throws them down one by one with contempt.*]

What! But this is ignoble! Horrible! Dreadful! What incompetence! What effrontery! They deserve to be beaten. Look! Look at my expression there! And this one gives me a false smile. Ha!

[*She tries to imitate the false smile by screwing up her face. When the last picture has been thrown down, she treads them underfoot as she walks off the barge.*]

My sedan!

[*Li directs it to be fetched immediately. She stalks in procession followed by the Emperor, the Empress, the Concubines, the Princess and the ladies, in dead silence. As she is about to enter the sedan, she turns and looks vindictively at the Emperor, who is now kneeling on the ground with the rest of the party.*]

Thank you for spoiling my birthday!

[*She is carried away, and the rest retire.*]

END OF SCENE ONE

[*Wen Li enters and says*]:

It is related of the Yellow Emperor, the earliest of the Sacred Mother's august Ancestors, that when asked what was the secret of success in war, he replied: 'Never fight on ground shaped like a tortoise on its back.' It has ever been uncertain what he meant by this dictum, but that it concealed a great truth has never been in doubt. Venerable dicta of this sort governed the Sacred Mother's military policy, and that She was able at the last to hand on in its entirety the Goodly Heritage to Her Successor, in spite of dangers both from within and from without, far exceeding those which confronted Her predecessors, proves that She knew their meaning and how to apply them.

As Her military policy was founded on the wisdom of the Sages, so also was Her civil administration made to conform to their precepts. Her nephew, the Emperor Kuang Hsu, whose deplorable lack of propriety in interrupting the celebration of Her birthday with business has been exposed in the last scene, was, alas! too dense to appreciate Her greatness. Misled by traitors, he thought that by disregarding tradition and introducing novelties he could confer benefits on the Great Pure Realm. But, as you will learn in the next scene, which takes place after an interval of four years, the Motherly and Auspicious thought otherwise and acted with her usual promptitude.

[*He bows and retires.*]

SCENE II

(The 5th of the 8th Moon, the twenty-fourth year of the reign of Kuang Hsu, September 20th, 1898.)

A private audience room, situated in the Palace of Heavenly Purity in the centre of the Great Within, is almost empty except for a small throne in the middle, a screen behind it and a few pots of flowers on stands. The early rays of the autumn sun are streaming in, and the fragrance of cassia flowers is carried on the soft breeze. His Majesty the Emperor Kuang Hsu is about to hold a private audience here and he comes in wearing his full court robes and headdress. Lately he has been greatly worried, and his face, his gait, and indeed his every movement indicate that he is distracted about some matter which he cannot—or dare not—decide. He comes forward with hesitating steps, followed by only one eunuch, and with puzzled eyes stares into space. He says absent-mindedly:

KUANG HSU. It is recorded of one of the greatest of our generals that on an occasion when he sought to ensure a victory he drew up his soldiers with a river behind them, burnt the bridges over it, sank his boats and destroyed his cooking pots, observing as he did so: 'Life comes to you only when death is hot at your heels.' But I wonder! I wonder!

[As he sits down on his throne, the Imperial Concubine, Pearl, enters, wearing an informal silk gown and with flowers in her hair, which is not covered with a headdress. With a self-possessed smile she approaches the Emperor and makes a bow to him.]

PEARL. Your Majesty should wonder no longer, for success or failure, life or death, entirely depend on your own efforts.

[He is delighted to see her and stretches out his hand to take hers. She comes near and sits down on the cushioned foot-rest in front of the Throne. This is done so naturally that she must certainly have sat there often before. Throughout this short episode she is holding his hand.]

KUANG HSU. I am so relieved you have come. I need your advice so badly.

PEARL. No, no, indeed you do not! For the past few months you have done a hundred things by yourself, and now the whole Empire, indeed, the whole world, is looking to you for the final stroke. And they know, and I know, that you will deal it.

KUANG HSU [*much reassured*]. When you are near me, Pearl, I feel so confident. But when I'm alone, I am never certain whether I'm right or wrong.

PEARL. But try and remember you *are* always right. The Emperor is incapable of making a mistake.

KUANG HSU. I'm afraid Her Majesty, the Empress Dowager, doesn't think so. She says she is always right and I'm always wrong . . .

PEARL. Well, she conducted the Japanese War, and we were defeated by the Dwarfs. Was she right then?

KUANG HSU. No, she was wrong.

PEARL. Then again, you wanted to reinforce Admiral Ting. Were you wrong?

KUANG HSU [*becoming animated*]. No, I was right!

PEARL. When she bought and destroyed the only railway built, was she right?

KUANG HSU. No, she was not!

PEARL. Well, then, when, in spite of her, you modernized the public examinations, ordered that science should be taught, introduced telegraphy, newspapers and telephones, equipped the army with modern weapons, were you wrong?

KUANG HSU. No. I know I was right. But actually it was the Reform Party who put all these things into my head.

PEARL. You are far too modest. They could never have done anything if it had not been for you. You saw that the Empress Dowager had to be resisted, if China were to advance. Though you knew she would be angry, you appointed Yuan Shih-Kai Inspector General of the Forces independent of her tool, Jung Lu, an act which has been acclaimed everywhere as a piece of great statesmanship.

KUANG HSU [*flattered and happy*]. You really think so? But I fear she will cancel my Edicts. Nobody can stop her if she decides to.

PEARL. *You* can and you must! The time has come for you to put an end to her power to interfere.

KUANG HSU [*anxiously*]. It sounds so simple, but tell me how?

PEARL. Assert your rightful authority! It's an outrage that she continues to usurp *your* power. If you act, the whole Court will support you—provided you show yourself strong enough to succeed.

KUANG HSU. But am I strong enough? For instance, Yuan Shih-Kai is coming this morning to thank me for the appointment, and I was advised by the Reformers to enlist his support. Will he support me? And will his support be enough? Advise me how to go about it.

PEARL. Certainly you are strong enough! With the well-armed division Yuan Shih-Kai controls, and it being handy so near Peking, his support will turn the scale. And of course he'll support you. He owes his position to you and will do anything you command.

KUANG HSU. Anything? Would he help me to retire the Dowager and to arrest the ruffians Jung Lu and Li Lien-Ying? Would he do that?

PEARL. Yes, he will. Promoted by you, he must back you; his future depends on it. But you must show resolution, or he will be afraid of your leaving him in the lurch when it comes to a clash.

KUANG HSU. You see things so clearly, Pearl. Tell me, how ought I to open the subject when he comes? Quick, he may be here any moment. I know what I'll do. I'll be very friendly with him. Talk without too much state, that's the main thing. Flatter him and offer him a chair . . .

PEARL. No, no! You must use the most formal Court language, and command him to occupy the Palace with his troops. The Imperial Guard and the eunuchs will be overawed. After that, it will be nothing to arrest Jung and Li, and then the Empress Dowager will be powerless.

KUANG HSU. It sounds easy when you say it. But suppose I don't impress him . . .

PEARL. Remember, you are the Son of Heaven. Command and you'll be obeyed.

[*A eunuch enters and kneels, announcing.*]

EUNUCH. His Excellency General Yuan Shih-Kai prays audience.

KUANG HSU. Quick, tell me what words I should use in commanding him! Quick! Quick! I mustn't keep him waiting.

[*He has become agitated.*]

PEARL. On the contrary! The longer you keep him waiting, the better. A man of Yuan's type who kicks his subordinates likes to be kicked by his superior. If you don't, he will not regard you as his superior. Be as stiff as you can, and all will be well. I will hide behind the screen, and if you forget to be yourself, I'll tap.

[*She goes behind the screen and the Emperor signs to the eunuch to admit Yuan. He is a short and stout soldier of forty and cultivates a very trustworthy face. When he approaches the Throne and kneels, he seems to be taller than he was a moment ago, for he has a big head, square shoulders, a long body but very short legs. He kow-tows.*]

YUAN. Your servant, Yuan Shih-Kai, Inspector-General of the Forces, pays his respects to Your Majesty.

KUANG HSU [*sitting stiffly upright*]. You have Our leave to speak.

YUAN. As the musketry course of my troops was ended, I took the opportunity of petitioning for an audience and, overwhelmed by Your Majesty's favour in promoting me, I come to tender my sincerest thanks.

KUANG HSU [*forgetting to play his part*]. For a matter of fact, it was the leaders of the Reform Party who . . .

[*A discreet tap is heard from behind the screen.*]
That is, We selected you from a number of nominations because We believed you knew more about modern arms than others of, perhaps, higher rank.

YUAN. Your Majesty is very gracious.

KUANG HSU. We attach great importance to reform in army matters, and if you justify Our selection [*lapsing again*] I shall try to obtain permission from . . .

[*Another tap is heard and the Emperor makes a visible effort.*]
I mean, We shall bestow on you the Yellow Riding Jacket.

YUAN. Your Majesty is too gracious. My poor abilities are entirely at Your Majesty's disposal.

KUANG HSU [*uneasily bending forward*]. Well, the thing is there was something I wanted you . . .

[*Another tap comes through and he immediately sits upright again and stiffens his tone.*]
When We granted this Audience, it was not solely to receive your thanks. We had in mind . . . in mind . . . In point of fact, I had . . .

[*Two taps are heard and he goes on with a rush of determination.*]
You are no doubt aware that there exists some opposition to the reforms which have recently been promulgated in our Edicts.

YUAN. Rumours of the kind have reached me, though I gave them no credit.

KUANG HSU. They are true, nevertheless, and it is in this connection that We have certain orders for you.

YUAN. Your Majesty has but to state them.

KUANG HSU [*with too patent relief*]. Really! Is that so? [*a tap*] Now, would you be prepared to—[*a louder tap*] That is . . . [*making a supreme effort*] The opposition to which We allude is centred in Li Lien-Ying, the Chief Eunuch, and Jung Lu, formerly Captain of the Imperial

Guard and now Viceroy of the Metropolitan Province. Both these individuals merit arrest and punishment, but owing to their influential positions and the forces at their disposal it would not be possible to apprehend them by ordinary judicial process.

[*He pauses, exhausted, and half turns towards the screen as if for support. Pearl gives him a gentle tap. He swallows, takes breath and continues.*]

We therefore command you to bring up your troops and surround the Purple Forbidden City, when opposition will collapse and the arrests can be effected without danger of resistance.

YUAN [*with over-emphasis*]. Your Majesty has conferred upon me an honour far greater than I could expect in choosing me for so important an undertaking. All my energies will be bent upon it and Your Majesty may rest assured that to bring it to a successful issue I would go to the Yellow Springs with a smile on my lips, even were my brains and liver to be trampled on the ground. With Your Majesty's permission I will now hasten to Tientsin, thence to rally my troops immediately to Your Majesty's support.

[*He kow-tows in an exaggerated manner and backs out. Pearl comes from behind the screen, looking uneasy. The Emperor takes hold of her hand and playfully pushes her into her old seat on the cushioned foot-rest. He is in high spirits, for he has never taken so definite a line before in his life.*]

KUANG HSU. Sit down, We command you! [*with a pleased smile*] I admit I was a little nervous at first, but I soon got into it. He was thoroughly impressed. Your tapping was a great help.

PEARL [*a little worried*]. You did well, and with a little practice will do better.

KUANG HSU. Don't you think it was all right?

PEARL. I'm not certain he was sincere. He protested his loyalty too much.

KUANG HSU [*still elated*]. Dare he disobey my orders?

PEARL. I wonder if he will come out in open support. He is such a time-server that if he doubts your courage to face the Dowager, he will do nothing.

KUANG HSU [*shaken, but trying to give himself courage*]. He wouldn't dare to betray me.

PEARL. Not if you act boldly now on your own initiative. Then he will join you.

KUANG HSU [*taking a breath*]. Tell me what to do and I'll do it.

PEARL [*solemnly*]. First, summon the Imperial Guard. Detail one detachment to arrest Jung Lu, who will be quite unprepared to resist. Then command the rest to accompany you to the Summer Palace. When there order them to sound the drum and mount your throne in the Main Hall, and decree the immediate arrest of Li.

KUANG HSU [swallowing repeatedly]. Yes? But supposing . . .

PEARL [seeing he is wavering]. Keep cool and repeat to yourself, 'I am the Son of Heaven, Mine is the power!'

KUANG HSU [shouting]. I am the Son of Heaven, Mine is the Power!

PEARL. You need not shout. But you must really feel it. Now, should the Dowager order you to get off the throne, you know what to do, don't you?

KUANG HSU [as if repeating a spell]. I am the Son of Heaven, Mine is the Power! I'll look at her firmly and command her to keep silence.

PEARL. Very good, indeed! Now, if she orders Li to drag you off, as Li has dragged and pushed you before, what then?

KUANG HSU [hypnotized]. That was only because I allowed it. As I am the Son of Heaven and Mine is the Power, how could he and his minions dare to approach me?

PEARL. Admirable! In a terrible voice you declare he is committing high treason. Then he will falter, and the Guardsmen will arrest him.

KUANG HSU. Yes, They're bound to. It's just a matter of will power, and now I know I have it. I am the Son of Heaven, Mine is the Power!

[He stands up and rehearses the gesture of giving an order.]

PEARL. Perfect! Perfect!

KUANG HSU [idiotically]. We command you to be silent!

[Just then a eunuch enters and kneels, announcing:]

EUNUCH. Prepare yourselves to receive Her Imperial Majesty the Empress Dowager.

KUANG HSU [looking at Pearl with terror in his eyes]. What?

PEARL [angrily]. Who is the Son of Heaven and whose is the Power?

KUANG HSU [sitting down majestically]. I am the Son of Heaven, Mine is the Power! [to eunuch] Show her in!

[The eunuch goes out stupefied.]

PEARL. Well done! Now sit squarely and demand her business.

[She gets up and he looks alarmed.]

KUANG HSU [hysterically]. Don't leave me! Hide again behind the screen.

[*Footsteps are heard and he grips the arms of the throne, addressing Pearl in a hoarse whisper.*]

Stand by me, Pearl, and tap, please! Tap . . . tap!

[*Hardly is Pearl behind the screen when Tzu Hsi enters, accompanied by Li Lien-Ying and Jung Lu, with a number of eunuchs and guards. She is astonished to see the Emperor sitting in state upon the throne. In a grating high voice, she addresses him.*]

TZU HSI. How dare you receive me seated! Get down and kneel.

[*He half rises, when there is a gentle tap and he sits again.*]

Kneel and kow-tow!

KUANG HSU [*murmuring*]. I am the Son of Heaven, Mine is the Power!

TZU HSI. What are you muttering?

KUANG HSU [*in a quaking voice*]. I am the Son of Heaven, Mine is the Power!

TZU HSI [*scarcely believing her ears*]. Have you lost your wits? You fool! You idiot!

[*Formidable and grim, she advances upon him, still seated but tightly clutching the arms of the throne. A gentle tap is followed by another. His lips move but it is impossible to hear what he is saying.*]

Do you know what you have committed?

KUANG HSU [*his stammer coming back*]. I have done n-n-nothing.

[*There is a tap, but it fails to reassure him, for he is visibly trembling.*]

TZU HSI. You have conspired!

[*So overpowering is the Dowager's personality that Kuang Hsu is convulsed with a feeling of guilt, as if what he had planned to do were, indeed, conspiracy. He is terrified.*]

KUANG HSU [*as if warding off a blow*]. N-n-n-no!

[*There are two sharp taps, but he does not hear them.*]

TZU HSI. You *have* conspired! And how wickedly! Since you were a child of four, I have lavished kindness and care on you. I clothed you, fed you, gave you wife and concubines, put you on the throne and gave you power. For twenty-four long years I have nursed and protected you. And now for all this your return is to plot my destruction!

KUANG HSU [*nearly in a state of collapse*]. I n-n-never . . .

[*A loud tap is followed by another, but Tzu Hsi's voice drowns it.*]

TZU HSI. You miserable fool! I know it's not your idea. You are incapable of having any ideas! You are only a tool in the hands of traitors who would fling you aside after they have used you. Don't you see that my fall to-day means yours to-morrow?

148

KUANG HSU [*burying his head in his hands*]. S-s-spare me!
[*There are several frantic taps from behind the screen and Tzu Hsi now hears them.*]

TZU HSI. What is that knocking? Li, go behind the screen and see.
[*Li goes to look. Pearl comes out of hiding with a dignified air and stands by the Emperor, holding his hand.*]
Ha! What were you doing there?

PEARL [*defiantly*]. I was in attendance on the Emperor. [*to Kuang Hsu*] Your Majesty, tell them you are the Son of Heaven, and that it is high treason to show you disrespect.

KUANG HSU [*brokenly*]. N-n-no!

TZU HSI [*contemptuously*]. Ha, ha! So this is your backbone! And she has been signalling to you! [*to Li*] Drag her away!
[*Li jerks his head and his eunuchs dart forward to drag Pearl away from the Emperor's side. She breaks loose and, in frantic rage and disdain, turns on the Empress Dowager.*]

PEARL. What is my crime? Nothing, except being faithful to the Emperor! What are your crimes? Usurpation, treason, robberies, murders, debaucheries. For forty years the whole world has been watching with horror. And now when a Son of Heaven . . . is about to . . . cleanse the Court . . . you force . . . your way . . . .
[*Before she can finish her words, the eunuchs have recaptured her and drag her away as she struggles and shouts. The Emperor rises from his seat and tries hesitatingly to stop the eunuchs, but finally gives it up. In the meantime Tzu Hsi has occupied the throne and he automatically kneels down before her, begging her to pardon the Pearl Concubine.*]

KUANG HSU. B-b-be gracious, Your Ma-Majesty, and s-spare her!

TZU HSI [*ignoring his words and looking at him in her calm but deadly fashion*]. When I handed over to you the power of the State and withdrew to my Summer Palace, hoping to rest after long labour, I little thought that I should be forced again to assume control. But my hopes have been shattered. The realm is in danger. I must take the reins again. You have become a nuisance and an encumbrance, and I will tell Li . . .
[*Li who is kneeling while he waits eagerly for the words, moistening his lips, as his wont is, a faithful, admiring, ferocious familiar, can contain himself no longer.*]

LI. Which one shall I do first, the girl or the Emperor?

KUANG HSU [*who is not entirely without nobler feelings*]. M-m-mercy

. . . .

149

TZU HSI [*with more contempt than before*]. No!

KUANG HSU [*getting out what he wanted to say*]. Do what you like to me-me, but s-s-spare her!

[*Li smiles and proceeds to take charge. But as he drags the Emperor away, Jung Lu intervenes by kneeling before Tzu Hsi.*]

JUNG LU. May I say a word . . . ?

TZU HSI [*with withering sarcasm*]. You are touched by their devotion to each other?

JUNG LU. No, Your Majesty. I am more practical. As it appears that the Emperor with his reform policy has a large following all over the Empire—nay, even the foreign devils are his admirers—it would be unwise for Your Majesty to act precipitately. Confine him, and also the Concubine.

[*Tzu Hsi frowns and Li looks menacingly at him.*]

At least, for the time being, pending Your Majesty's final decision in the case and the reaction of the country.

TZU HSI [*violently*]. The country is all right. The people don't want this nonsense of reforms. And the foreign devils . . . [*reflecting an instant*] Well?

JUNG LU. I recommend that His Majesty the Emperor be conducted to the Ocean Terrace in the Imperial Lakes and be confined there until his followers are extirpated and . . .

TZU HSI. Until his health is better . . . or worse!

[*Li smiles at the last word, and relaxes his hold, looking happily at her.*] Li, conduct the Emperor to his confinement!

LI. Yes, Old Ancestor!

[*He jerks his head contemptuously and leaves such a minor job to be done by his minions. Two eunuchs take away the Emperor who is now reduced to semi-idiocy.*]

TZU HSI. Now Jung Lu, as a reward for your efficient handling of this day's work and for your cautious advice, I am elevating you to the Privy Council and giving you leave to wear the red button.

JUNG LU [*kow-towing*]. Your Majesty's gracious benevolence is without stint or term.

TZU HSI. Your first duty as a member of the Council will be to announce the following Mandate from His Majesty the Emperor Kuang Hsu.

JUNG LU [*who is a little slow*]. From His Majesty the Emperor?

TZU HSI. So it appears. It is to this effect. [*pursing her lips*] 'The times through which the country is passing are full of difficulty, and though We have laboured unremittingly at Our task We are not satisfied that Our efforts have been crowned with success. In Our eagerness to bring the administration up-to-date We have given undue weight to foreign concoctions and are alarmed to observe the confusion which has resulted. On more than one occasion We besought Her Imperial Majesty the Empress Dowager to leave Her retirement and undertake again the government. She refused, but chaos increasing and Our health being seriously affected We renewed Our entreaties and She has now graciously condescended to grant Our prayer. From this day forward Her Majesty will transact all public business and We Ourselves, at the head of Our Princes and Ministers, will perform obeisance before Her in the Hall of Diligent Government. The words of the Emperor.'

[*She retires, followed by the rest.*]

END OF SCENE TWO

[*Wen Li enters and says*]:

After the Holy Mother had admonished the Emperor and sent him to meditate on his errors in the Ocean Terrace, She employed Her energies to bring back the Celestial Empire to the Way of the Ancestors. In this She was supported by the people, many of whom banded themselves together into a society called the Righteous Harmonious Fists, or, for short, the Boxers. This Society, no less than She, desired to be rid of the Foreign Devils, who not only had forced their hairy presence upon the Heavenly City in the persons of their Ambassadors, but were causing uproar in the country towns with their merchants and missionaries.

It is written in the Book of Songs:
'If soft, chew it,
    If hard, spit it out.'

The Holy Mother for long had sought to chew the Red Barbarians, that is to say, to assimilate them harmlessly into the body of the State. But now their numbers and presumption increasing, this method of dealing with them was no longer efficacious, and in the twenty-sixth year of the reign of Kuang Hsu, that is the devil year 1900, She decided to spit them out of Her mouth.

[*He bows and retires.*]

SCENE III

(The 21st of the 5th Moon, the twenty-sixth year of the reign of Kuang Hsu, June 15th, 1900.)

The Eastern Audience Hall of the Palace of Ceremonial Phoenixes in the Purple Forbidden City is prepared for the meeting of the Grand Council at which the most important decision of the Dynasty is to be made. Two Chairs of State with desks are placed a little distance from each other at one end of the Hall. The rest of the place is practically empty, except for a few large pots of flowers of the summer season. These are ranged in stands in the corners and along the walls of the Hall.

Her Majesty, the Empress Dowager Tzu Hsi, dressed in full Court robes, enters with Li and four other eunuchs. Though it is only two years since we had the honour of seeing Her Majesty last, it is clear the Motherly Countenance has greatly aged. State affairs are always burdensome, but lately she has had to cope with problems of exceptional gravity. No wonder she looks worried and tired.

TZU HSI [*as she crosses to her place*]. A poet once remarked that he aspired neither to be monarch of this nor of the other world, for he had no inclination to punish the wicked and found the troubles of the common people only a bother.

[*She sits on the bigger Chair on the left, while Li and the other eunuchs stand behind her. Jung Lu follows almost immediately and kneels before her. He is in full court dress and wears the red button.*]

JUNG LU. Your slave, the Grand Secretary, Jung Lu, craves Your Majesty's pardon for coming before the others. But the occasion is so urgent that he must speak out. Since the Boxers quarrelled with the foreign missionary people, he has done his best to avoid a clash. But this is no longer possible.

TZU HSI. We told the world that We regret the death of the missionaries, though, in fact, We have no sympathy for them. Inform Us now frankly how the situation stands between Us and the Barbarians. Speak openly and without fear of angering Us. Is there chance of compromise?

JUNG LU. No chance whatever, Your Majesty. I heard from reliable sources that the Barbarian Legations are about to present four demands. First, that the Emperor should leave the Palace, where now he enjoys Your Majesty's protection, and proceed to what they have the effrontery to term a safe place in which they may negotiate with him. Second, that the customs be collected under their supervision, and third, that our troops be commanded by their officers in a campaign to suppress the Boxers. Finally, and most shocking of all, that Your Majesty go into exile.

TZU HSI [*very angry in spite of herself*]. Then what I always believed has come true. The foreigners' object is to eat China!

JUNG LU. But Your Majesty will know how to send them away hungry.

TZU HSI. They shall not get a bite! What vermin! Well has it been said: 'Give a rat shelter and he will eat you out of house!' When my back is turned, they seduce the Emperor with the help of the Reformers. Then when I place him in detention, they declare they are accredited not to me but to him, and showing a ludicrous solicitude for his health, as if I were not watching over him and the Grand Physician were incompetent, offer to send their quack doctors to prescribe for him. Vermin! Rats! And after my appointment of an Heir Apparent, they spread malicious rumours which have been readily believed by ill-disposed persons, so that I have to provide that Chair [*pointing to the Chair and desk near her*] merely to let the Emperor be seen, otherwise people will say I have murdered him. Ah! here he comes whom they thought put away.

[*Kuang Hsu enters more dead than alive, attended by his eunuchs. Terribly nervous and brow-beaten, he hastens forward to kneel before his ruthless aunt.*]

KUANG HSU. My respects to Your Majesty.

TZU HSI [*briefly*]. Take your seat.

[*Kuang Hsu rises and slinks wretchedly to his Chair of State.*]
Li, tell the Council to come in.

LI [*calling*]. Your Highnesses, Your Excellencies, all arise, if you please!

[*The Princes and high officials have been waiting outside the Hall kneeling. They rise and file in, each dressed in his full court robes, most of them wearing coral but a few sapphire buttons. His Highness, Yi Kuan, the Prince Ching, the senior member of the Imperial Clan, is their leader. He is elderly and has an amiable and stupid face. As soon as they have knelt down in two rows before the Thrones, the Prince Ching, on behalf of them all, says loudly.*]

慶親王奕劻

PRINCE CHING—HEAD OF THE IMPERIAL
CLAN
(He is elderly and has an amiable and stupid face)

CHING. Your slave, Yi Kuan, the Prince Ching, and the other members of the Imperial Clan, together with the Grand Secretaries of the Privy Council, the Members of the Six Boards and of the Nine Ministries, pay our respects to Your Majesties.

[*They make a kow-tow in unison. Then Tzu Hsi, in a grand and formal manner, addresses them.*]

TZU HSI. We have summoned you to this extraordinary meeting because the Empire is faced with the greatest crisis in its history. For forty years, since the Barbarians burnt Our Palaces, their presumption has continued to increase, till now the whole realm has been thrown into confusion. We have always been indulgent to them and shown it by granting them audience without insisting on the ritual kow-tow, which has heretofore been obligatory. This indulgence was proper. Just as We pardon an animal for not knowing how to pay its respects, so did We pardon the Red Barbarians. But as soon as they gain an inch, they advance a foot. For their progress in their insolent design to disrupt the Government and destroy Our ancient civilization, you, gentlemen, must bear a heavy responsibility, for you did not check in good time the madmen who style themselves Reformers, and who are the Barbarians' accomplices.

[*The Princes and Ministers kow-tow once more.*]

Therefore We have called you, for as it was your duty to have prevented what has befallen, so now are you bound to prescribe the remedy. Be open and frank, that you earn Our commendation.

[*There is silence for a moment, then a comparatively young official speaks in a loud and agitated voice.*]

YUAN. Your servant, Yuan Chang, the Minister of Sacrifice, begs to observe that we must also examine into our own faults, and not entirely blame the Barbarians. The Boxers are bandits and since their entrance into the Capital, the common people no longer respect the law. Many of them have joined the bandits and begun to murder the Chinese Christians. Tung Fu-Shiang, the Moslem General, is the man to wipe out the Boxers and restore order.

TUAN. Your slave, Tsai Yi, the Prince Tuan, proclaims this to be the right method and heartily congratulates the able Minister on his suggestion! [*pointing his thumb upwards in a sarcastic manner*] It will immediately lose us the support of the people! The Boxers alone can drive out the Barbarians. And a rebellion is certain if the Boxers are suppressed.

TZU HSI. What then, in your opinion, is the proper course to pursue?

TUAN. Your Majesty, the Legations have already sent for help and a relief force is expected any time from the coast. We must act before it arrives. As Your Majesty is aware, our troops are scattered about the Empire.

JUNG LU. I have already telegraphed to the Southern provinces for troops . . .

TUAN [*impatiently*]. But before they can be assembled the Barbarians will be upon us. The Boxers are handy and may be used in the emergency. When the Barbarians see the Legations have been taken, they will not dare to send a relief force.

CHAO. Your servant, Chao Shu-Chiao, the President of the Board of Punishments, begs to second the proposal, and ventures to suggest that His Highness, Tsai Shun, the Prince Chuan, and His Excellency Kang Yi, the Grand Secretary, be appointed commanders of the righteous people known as the Boxers, and launch the attack on the Barbarian Legations.

PU KUO. Your slave, Tsai Lan, the Duke Pu Kuo, begs to second the proposal.

SHU [*an old official*]. Your servant, Shu Chin-Chen, Vice President of the Board of Civil Office, begs to point out that even if the Legations are taken and all the barbarian garrison is killed, the matter will not end there. The foreign nations will organize a punitive force and our Ancestral Altars will be levelled to the ground.

YUAN. According to our own laws of war, envoys must be treated with respect. To attack the Legations is to act against all international usage. The Boxers should not be employed and we should be careful not to start an armed conflict.

LI SAN [*an old Confucian scholar*]. Your slave, Li San, President of the Board of Finance, begs to suggest that if a polite request be sent to the Red Barbarian commander, Admiral Sey-Mou, not to despatch a relief force, he will comply with it. For a Foreign Devil he is known to have a strong sense of propriety and, were it not for his colour, he might be described as a gentleman.

TUAN [*furious*]. You traitor! You are a Secondary Hairy Devil!

TZU HSI [*slowly*]. This is hardly to the point. Let us face the facts. Our fortifications in Ta-ku have been taken by the Barbarians and news has just come in that they are demanding the seizure of Our revenues, the control of Our army and, above all, the handing over to them of His Majesty, the Emperor! No doubt you will agree that it is now time for drastic action.

[*This news obviously startles the members of the Council.*]

There confronts you, gentlemen, a great decision. Is there any alternative to war? If not, should the righteous Boxers be used? These are the questions you must answer, and history will hold you responsible if you answer them wrongly.

MOST OF THE OFFICIALS. Such demands must be rejected! Yes, yes! Rejected!

TZU HSI. You have not answered Our questions. Do you or do you not advise war?

CHING. It will be seemly to give the Legations an opportunity to leave even if war is declared. If they do not leave, let them be driven out by the Boxers.

TZU HSI [*quickly*]. We accept that advice, which We conceive to be sound and in accordance with Our usual indulgence. Therefore, We appoint the Prince Chuan and the General Secretary Kang Yi as the joint commanders-in-chief of the Righteous People's Force. An ultimatum will be sent to the Legations, giving them till to-morrow to lower their flags and be gone. If they remain, they must bear the consequences.

KUANG HSU [*faintly*]. The gravity of the s-s-situation calls for de-de-deliberation. We cannot a-afford to s-s-start war. The fate of the Empire is at s-s-stake . . .

TZU HSI [*angrily*]. War has already been started by them. The Empire is confronted with subjugation. If, as you propose, we bow to those who have come to enslave us, with what face shall we meet our Sainted Ancestors by the Yellow Springs? To fight and lose is at least better than to sit waiting to lose!

HSU [*a very old gentleman*]. Your servant, Hsu Yun-Yi, President of the Board of War, begs to point out that for war we must have the whole Empire behind us. Now I have received a telegram urging the Council to maintain peace at all costs and it is signed by Their Excellencies, Li Hung-Chang, Viceroy of the Two Kwangs, Liu Kuan-Yi, Viceroy of the Two Kiangs, Chang Chih-Tung, Viceroy of the Two Hus, Shu Yin-Kwei, Viceroy of Fukien, together with the Governors of Kiangsu, Anhwei, Hupeh, Hunan, Kwangtung and the Inspector on the Yangtze River. His Excellency, Yuan Shih-Kai, Governor of Shantung, also wired to me that he cannot see his way to send his forces North except it be for the suppression of the

Boxer bandits. We should not ignore the opinion of the south half of the Empire.

LI PING-HENG [*a big soldier*]. Your servant Li Ping-Heng, the Inspector on the Yangtze River, has just arrived in the Capital after receiving Imperial orders. I have not signed such a telegram!

[*A ripple of amazement passes over the assembly.*]

JUNG LU. I, too, have recently been in telegraphic communication with his Excellency Yuan Shih-Kai, Governor of Shantung, and he is, as he has ever been, loyal to Their Majesties.

YUAN. There are always some people who can bore from both ends. The Governor of Shantung is one and the Grand Secretary Jung Lu is another. Some of us have seen a copy of the Grand Secretary's communication. It was addressed, not to Yuan Shih-Kai, but through him to the Viceroys and Governors of the South who want peace. In it he requests them to do nothing should war be declared in the North!

[*Several of those present exclaim: 'Traitor', and Tzu Hsi looks piercingly at Jung Lu, who remains perfectly calm.*]

JUNG LU. When a country is in confusion, documents are sometimes unreliable. I confess I did send the Viceroys a telegram by care of Governor Yuan, but evidently it was altered by some ill-disposed persons. I take this opportunity to report to Your Majesty that the same thing happened with the Imperial Edict sent to the Governors, in which Your Majesty ordered the execution of all the offending missionaries and their followers. Several Governors found the word 'execution' altered to 'protection'.

TZU HSI [*in her terrifying voice*]. I charge you to find out who are the traitors who did this!

JUNG LU. A report has just reached me that such altered Edicts were despatched by Their Excellencies Yuan Chang and Shu Chin-Chen, the Minister of Sacrifice and the Vice-President of the Board of Civil Office.

[*Several people cry 'Treason!' Tzu Hsi looks at Shu and Yuan.*]

TZU HSI. Have you anything to say?

YUAN. I did it for the sake of the country.

SHU. And I did it for the sake of humanity.

[*Tzu Hsi turns and looks at Li, who is hovering at her elbow, like a bird of prey which scents carrion.*]

TZU HSI. Li, conduct these two gentlemen out . . .

LI [*with happy anticipation*]. Yes, All-Mighty?

TZU HSI. And deliver them to the Board of Punishments, to be tried for treason and executed in public without undue delay.

LI [*with a balked look on his evil face*]. Yes, All-Mighty.

YUAN AND SHU [*kow-towing*]. We thank Your Majesty for the honour.

[*Li jerks his head and two eunuchs conduct Yuan and Shu out. They maintain their dignity.*]

TZU HSI. Is there anybody else who votes against war?

[*She scans the crowd threateningly and all tremble.*]

LIEN. Your slave, Lien Yuan, Grand Secretary and member of the Privy Council, begs to inquire whether it would not suffice to serve the ultimatum upon France alone? It was the misbehaviour of her Catholic priests which roused the people in the first instance. Why should China, and, I ask, can China, fight twelve nations at once?

KANG. Your slave, Kang Yi, Grand Secretary, begs to point out that though to take arms against the barbarian world would be futile did we depend upon earthly means alone, it is feasible because the righteous Boxers are magicians.

HSU. As the President of the Board of War, I submit that in all our military past no record exists of an army winning a victory by magic.

LI SAN. Besides, the Boxers have no magical powers.

TZU HSI [*in a judicious tone*]. We will not permit a wrangle at this stage of the proceedings on the efficacy of magic in the field of battle. We may not depend upon magic, but may we not depend upon the confidence of the people? Certainly, if you go into the streets and inquire of any passer-by, he will tell you that the Barbarians must be driven away and that the Boxers are the only instruments to do it. Now if such is the popular opinion and you go against it, the Government will forfeit the confidence of the people. Our strength is not great, and if We lose public confidence We shall lose soon afterwards the Mandate of Heaven.

JUNG LU [*unctuously*]. Your Majesty speaks like the Sages of old.

TZU HSI [*piously*]. That We did! Yet, have We spoken with such wisdom as Heaven has vouchsafed to Us, and now, with the sanction of Our Council here present, We declare for war. But war is incalculable, and if, in spite of our taking arms, the Ancestral Altars cannot be protected from calamity, you gentlemen will bear witness to Our untiring efforts for peace, nor will blame Us, alleging that after three hundred years of glory the Great Pure Dynasty was brought to ruin by an Empress Dowager.

[*Many kow-tow and voice their support, though some remain silent.*]

I now appoint Their Excellencies Hsu Yun-Yi, the President of the Board of War, Li San, President of the Board of Finance, and Lien Yuan, Grand Secretary and Member of the Privy Council, to carry the ultimatum to the Legations.

HSU. While deeply sensible of the honour conferred upon me, I submit that I am hardly qualified, being unconnected with the Foreign Affairs Yamen and having had no dealings with the Barbarians.

TZU HSI. No dealings? Was it not you who conducted their Embassy staffs on a tour of the Summer Palace? We know you are friendly with them. [*addressing all three*] Proceed at once. There is no time to lose.

[*Before leaving, the Emissaries first kow-tow to Tzu-Hsi and then to the Emperor, who reaches out and catches Hsu Yun-Yi by the sleeve. He looks desperate.*]

KUANG HSU. Wait! We are taking an irrevocable s-s-step that may plunge the country into a hopeless conflict. Ministers t-t-talk glibly of war, but in the Jap-ap-apanese war, for which everybody v-voted, we were totally de-defeated. But the Allied European na-nations are ten . . . a hundred . . . a thou-thousand times stronger than Jap-ap-Japan. If we defy them we are do-doomed.

TZU HSI [*raising her voice in anger*]. Let them go, Emperor!

[*He lets go his hold and sinks back in his seat weeping. Hsu Yun-Yi sobs and wipes his tears, trying to hold the Emperor's hand.*]

Hsu Yun-Yi must not act in an outrageous manner. Go at once. The Emperor cannot stop you, for it is the will of the Council, which does not wish, like him, the country's humiliation.

[*As the three are going, she addresses Jung Lu.*]

Depute a company of the Imperial Guard to protect them in case the Barbarians seek to murder them, and double the Guards about the Palace. Send expresses to Our commanders in the South to hasten to Us with all their troops.

JUNG LU. The Southern armies are too distant and may not arrive in time, but I have sent an express to Governor Yuan of Shantung.

TZU HSI [*to the Council*]. You see, gentlemen, all measures are taken that Our foresight can suggest.

YUN. Your servant, Yun Yui-Ting, the Grand Historiographer,

has a submission to make. There remains one measure to be taken. In the history of the Tang Dynasty it is recorded that before the Empress Wu went to war she always directed that her Phoenix Chariot, which was used then as now for provincial tours of inspection, be kept in instant readiness outside the Palace Gates, so that she could leave the Capital, if necessity arose, without impropriety. It seems to your servant that this course might be followed by Your Majesty.

TZU HSI [*angrily*]. We understand your insinuation! You are very impertinent!

YUN [*calmly*]. I was merely quoting an historical precedent as in duty bound as Court Historian.

TZU HSI [*impatiently*]. Enough! The Council is adjourned.

[*They all kow-tow and file out except Jung Lu who remains behind.*]

Come here, Jung Lu. What did you mean by those private communications with the traitors in the South? I hope the accusations are groundless.

JUNG LU [*who knows explanations and excuses are no good with her*]. There is a saying of the Sages: 'A wise man must save himself whatever happens', and I ventured to make sure, for the sake of the Old Ancestor, that even if the North is rendered uninhabitable, there will be somewhere for the Old Ancestor to go to.

TZU HSI [*reflecting for a second*]. Yes, and I think you had better get some water melons and other refreshments and have them sent to the besieged Legations. It may be worth while. You never can tell.

JUNG LU. The Old Ancestor is sagacious. But there is one point on which I seek enlightenment: why should I depute a company of Guards to protect three men whom the Old Ancestor has sent to their certain death—for I presume the Barbarians will shoot them at once?

TZU HSI [*smiling*]. You are sometimes dense, Jung Lu. If they are lucky enough to slip out of the tiger's den, they will be in safe hands to be turned over to the Board of Punishments and tried for high treason on the charge of accepting bribes from our enemies, a reasonable presumption or they would not have spoken against war in the way they did.

JUNG LU. I understand. And I will see that evidence is provided.

TZU HZI. And see also that they are condemned and executed.

LI [*apprehensively*]. Executed?

TZU HSI. Why not, Li? Are they your friends?

LI [*who fears that his job of private executioner will be ruinously en-croached upon if these legal trials and executions are to become the rule*]. No, no! But if the Old Ancestor continues to make use of the machinery of the law, my work will be gone and I shall have to crave permission to retire.

[*Tzu Hsi smiles and they leave the hall.*]

END OF SCENE THREE

[Wen Li enters and says]:

Critics of Her Majesty have been known to suggest that Her policy in dealing with the Boxer uprising was a failure and that the war She declared against the whole world ended in a fiasco. But those of you who have followed judiciously the last scene will have perceived that the decision was taken according to the express wish of the Grand Council, and will, therefore, allow that the Council was entirely responsible. No doubt, had the policy succeeded, the members would have taken the credit to themselves, and when it did not, they put the blame on Her Majesty.

Even if it is thought that She had indeed some hand in it, the truth may well be that the Motherly and Auspicious directed the Boxers not to press home the assault, from a desire that Her indulgence be made manifest to the Barbarians and that, dazzled by Her inexhaustible forbearance, they might lay down their arms and go peacefully their ways. For such was ever Her heavenly benevolence towards Her unfortunate subjects in the Outer Regions, whom, deprived of the felicity of residence in the Celestial Empire, She deemed to be worthy of the utmost commiseration.

As to the so-called flight of Her Majesty which followed two months afterwards, the next scene will disclose how it came about and that it was in reality a calculated withdrawal designed to cause to the Barbarians loss of face.

[He bows and retires.]

SCENE IV

(The 21st of the 7th Moon, the twenty-sixth year of the reign of Kuang Hsu, August 15th, 1900.)

The palace prison in which the Imperial Concubine Pearl has been detained during the last two years is merely one of the many houses in the Forbidden City. The stage now represents its courtyard. There is little to be seen except a few big pottery tubs, in which lotus flowers are growing. Along one wall are clumps of bamboos, and their grace will not have been lost upon the Imperial Concubine, for she was a reader of poetry and well acquainted with Su Tung-Po's famous line:

> Better to eat a meal without meat than to live in a place without bamboos.

At first her imprisonment, like the Emperor's on the Ocean Terrace island, was strictly enforced, but latterly, as in his case also, it has been somewhat relaxed, with the result that she is not entirely ignorant of what has been happening, though naturally a little behind with the news. The courtyard is empty. Suddenly the Emperor Kuang Hsu is seen to hurry in unannounced, dressed in an ordinary silk gown and summer hat. He is accompanied by one eunuch. He looks harassed.

KUANG HSU. An Emperor's life in wartime is far worse than a dog's in peace.

[*He looks about. There is no one to be seen. The eunuchs who should have been on duty at the gate have left their posts. His own eunuch now calls loudly.*]

EUNUCH. The Lord of Ten Thousand Years deigns to call on Your Highness.

[*Pearl comes rushing out with surprise and joy on her face, followed at some distance by a maid. Two years' imprisonment have not impaired her beauty. Dressed in an ordinary silk gown and her hair not properly done, she is even more attractive than when we last saw her. She approaches the Emperor and smilingly kneels at his feet.*]

PEARL. Your Majesty! What happiness to see you after these two long years.

KUANG HSU [*in an adoring voice*]. It seems far more than that to me.

[*He sits down and takes her hand, as she stands looking tenderly at him.*]

PEARL. Is Your Majesty well? Oh, I am so happy! I have dreamed of this. Maybe, I am only dreaming.

KUANG HSU. When I awoke this morning I hoped it was only a dream.

PEARL. What do you mean?

KUANG HSU. Have you not heard? The whole Palace is in the utmost confusion. My guards have fled and neither do I see any signs of yours. Otherwise I could never have got here.

PEARL. Why, what has happened?

KUANG HSU. It was reported last night that the barbarian relief force was within a few miles of the city. The Empress Dowager summoned the Council no less than five times yesterday and has ordered her Phoenix Chariot to be ready to take her to the frontier. There was some delay, for the grooms had deserted, but as soon as the carriages are ready we start. I suspected that nobody would inform you, and that is why I have come. You must get ready to go with me, for when the barbarian soldiery break in they will loot, burn, rape . . .

PEARL [*who has remained calm*]. It is very old-fashioned to talk of Barbarians. Your Majesty has too good an understanding of the European powers to speak of them so. Their leaders are not barbarians, and, as for looting and raping, if you can get in touch with them at once, there will be none of that. You have a great opportunity, if you act promptly.

KUANG HSU. *I* act?

PEARL. Yes, Your Majesty can do it all by yourself. [*signalling to her maid*] Bring the Court robe to me at once.

[*The maid goes quickly.*]

KUANG HSU. What Court robe?

PEARL. The one you wore on the day we were parted. I managed to get it and kept it as a memento and now it will be useful. As the Empress Dowager is going away, why not stay in Peking yourself, receive the foreign Ambassadors and Commanders, and restore order? Meet them and come to terms with them. That can still be done. It is not too late.

KUANG HSU. But would they negotiate with me? Now that we have set the savage Boxers on them, they will want revenge.

PEARL. But everyone knows you had no hand in that. The foreigners will not harm you. Surely you are not afraid of them?

165

KUANG HSU. No, I'm not, certainly nothing like as afraid of them as of the Empress Dowager!

PEARL. Then set out at once for the Legations. A man with a white flag of truce can go in front of you. When they see your dragon robe—that is why you must wear it—they will know that the Emperor himself is coming to meet them. They will feel honoured and be delighted. You will be received with every distinction . . .

KUANG HSU [*moved by her words*]. If I do it, it will not be for myself . . .

PEARL. But by doing it you will save the city from fire and looting. You can ask the Ambassadors and Commanders to stop their soldiers from entering the City.

[*The maid brings the robe and Pearl starts to put it on the Emperor, who now stands up. As she helps him to dress, he looks at her with gratitude and admiration.*]

Be calm and dignified. You can save the country, save the Dynasty and save hundreds, perhaps thousands of lives. Now you are properly attired, you must set out to meet their leaders before their men start to attack the City. A peace can be signed, and then the whole nation will bless you. And the more intelligent members of the Government will flock to you. The Empress Dowager will be deserted. Where she is will be of no matter. Her evil reign will be at an end. A new era will dawn for China.

KUANG HSU [*as always, transformed by her words*]. Good Pearl, you have put courage into me. I'll do it! I'll go! I shall be free! I feel I am no longer afraid of the Empress Dowager!

EUNUCH [*at the gate*]. Prepare yourselves to receive Her Imperial Majesty, the Empress Dowager.

[*The Emperor is petrified. Pearl, though startled, still retains command of herself. There is an awful silence for a second when the formidable shape of Tzu Hsi appears in the gateway. Unlike the others, she is in her court robe and wearing her high headdress. She comes stalking into the courtyard and the Emperor finds his knees bending in spite of himself. Pearl is alarmed and tears rush from her eyes. After what happened on the last occasion when she was with the Emperor she has not much hope of getting him to act with decision. But she is not going to give up. This time Tzu Hsi is alone. She has no guards. The redoubtable Li is not with her. And the Palace is in confusion. So stopping Kuang Hsu from kneeling with a quick pull, Pearl whispers earnestly in his ear.*]

PEARL. Keep calm and dignified! Tell her, tell her boldly and confidently that you know a way of saving the city, the government, the country and even herself—and don't kneel down!

KUANG HSU [*momentarily encouraged*]. All right.

[*By this time the Empress Dowager is in the centre of the courtyard and the Emperor, making a great effort, stands at some distance from her and makes a stiff bow. He tries to say his lines, but it is the Empress Dowager who speaks first. Her voice is calm and cold.*]

TZU HSI. Li was correct. You *are* here! Have I disturbed your love-making?

KUANG HSU [*bravely*]. No, Your Majesty. For I came here on business of s-s-state and now I am g-going to s-s-see the foreigners. I will s-save the city, and s-s-save the country . . . and s-s-save Your Majesty.

TZU HSI [*really astonished*]. What!

[*The Emperor is immediately cowed and stands there looking at Pearl for help.*]

PEARL. His Majesty believes that, were he to go personally to the Legations and see the foreign leaders, a parley could be arranged and the city spared the horrors of a sack.

TZU HSI [*witheringly*]. Magnificent! And what will be Our position?

[*She sits on the chair vacated by the Emperor.*]

PEARL [*pleading*]. Your Majesty has nothing whatever to fear. If His Majesty agrees to punish the Boxer leaders and those who have backed them, the foreigners will be appeased.

TZU HSI [*with bitter contempt*]. I see. A most interesting proposal! A very pretty scheme! And I wonder who put it into his head? It sounds too bold for his invention. [*to the Emperor*] Come here and kneel down. Tell me who . . .

PEARL [*seeing the Emperor is giving in, urgently in a whisper*]. Start out, Your Majesty! Not a moment is to be lost. There is nothing to keep you here. Leave me to deal with her.

[*The Emperor starts to go. Tzu Hsi, with a grim face, stands up and raises her hand.*]

TZU HSI. Stop! I command you!

PEARL. Your Majesty cannot stop the Emperor. While His Majesty goes to meet the foreigners, I am here to answer for him.

[*Tzu Hsi glances about her. She perceives that she can count on no support from the Emperor's eunuch. She is isolated for the moment and has no way of forcing her will on Pearl and stopping the Emperor. For a few seconds she does not know what to do. The Emperor, perceiving that she is balked by Pearl's indomitable spirit, recovers his presence of mind and starts again for the gate. But suddenly a startling image is seen through the gateway. It is the gross figure of Li Lien-Ying. With heavy steps he comes running and leans on the gate-post to recover his breath. As if he had seen an apparition, the Emperor turns back trembling, his face ashen white. Tzu Hsi, thus reassured, sits back in her seat with composure.*]

TZU HSI. You have come in time! I have a little job for you.

LI [*panting*]. Yes—Old—Ancestor, I thought you must—have come here. I ran—all the way.

TZU HSI [*kindly*]. Poor old man! So devoted. Come in and rest a little. Don't stand on ceremony. This is quite a family occasion.

LI. Thank you, Old Ancestor.

[*He comes in, glancing contemptuously at the Emperor and Pearl.*]

But Your Majesty spoke of a little job. That will do me more good than resting. Which of them is it to be? Both this time, I hope.

[*With a sinister smile he goes up to the Emperor. Pearl, pointing her finger at him, cries.*]

PEARL. It is high treason to lay hands on the Emperor.

LI [*not impressed*]. Is it? I never heard that before.

TZU HSI. Not so fast, Li! Leave the Emperor alone. But conduct Her Highness away.

LI [*laying hold of Pearl*]. Yes, Old Ancestor.

[*Just then there is a commotion outside the gate and two eunuchs, rushing in, kneel inside the gateway. One of them calls out.*]

EUNUCH. His Excellency, the Grand Secretary, Jung Lu, urgently craves audience.

TZU HSI. Let him come in.

[*But before she has finished her words, Jung Lu has already run in. He appears to be panic-stricken and flings himself down before her.*]

What is it?

JUNG LU. Your Majesty, the Foreign Devils have broken into the Southern City! Strange-looking soldiers are reported in the Temple of Heaven.

TZU HSI [*firm and cool*]. You may be alarming yourself unnecessarily. They are probably Tartar levies, the vanguard of the Moslem general, who has been ordered to enter the city to protect Us.

JUNG LU [*despair in his voice*]. Unfortunately, no, Your Majesty! The Moslem General is fleeing westwards!

TZU HSI [*wholly calm and collected*]. In—that—case—we—leave.

[*By this time there is a small crowd of eunuchs in the gateway and at Tzu Hsi's last word, they seem thrown into confusion. Li, too, has lost his self-possession, but not his devotion to his mistress. He forgets about Pearl, and goes to Tzu Hsi.*]

LI. The Old Buddha must not linger for another second!

[*Pearl has been watching the Empress Dowager and Jung Lu all the time. Grasping the situation rapidly, she sees there is a last chance. She goes to the Emperor and says to him in a whisper.*]

PEARL. Go now, there is no one to stop you! Have courage and think of your great Ancestors!

[*These words seem to galvanize the Emperor and he starts to go towards the gate. Tzu Hsi looks on, a sneer on her lips, with Li beside her, awaiting her pleasure.*]

TZU HSI. Come back! Are you so simple as to believe I will let you take matters out of my hands? You must think me very stupid if you imagine I will allow them to make a tool of you to destroy me. No! Wherever I go, you shall come with me. Let them loot and burn Peking as they did the old Summer Palace. I shall build it again when they have gone.

[*The Emperor stops and looks at Pearl for help. She approaches the Empress Dowager, kneels, and appeals to her with tears in her eyes.*]

PEARL. I appeal to Your Majesty, think of your people! For the sake of your people, let him go! For the sake of the country, let him go! For the sake of humanity, let him go!

TZU HSI. People and humanity! We have heard such terms before! And we know how to answer those who use them.

[*She looks meaningly at Li, who nods and smiles, his old creased face darkly happy. She turns to Pearl again.*]

I warned you not to interfere with what did not concern you. You disobeyed my warning, and I shut you up here, holding my hand indulgently, though your life was forfeit. Now you have disobeyed me once more. It is too much. It is the end. [*to Li*] Be good enough to conduct Her Highness on the first stage of her journey to the Yellow Springs!

[*Li makes a sign with glad alacrity and his minions seize Pearl and drag her away. The Emperor kneels before the Empress Dowager and sobs aloud. He cringes on the ground like a beaten dog, listening to the footsteps of the woman he adores growing fainter as she goes to her death.*]

JUNG. Delay no longer, Old Ancestor. There is not a moment to lose.

TZU HSI. I am ready.

[*With a quick movement she discards her imperial robe and discloses herself dressed in the blue clothes of a peasant woman. She also removes her head-dress and her hair appears beneath brushed back and tied in a single knot. Jung Lu looks at her aghast. She smiles.*]

You are astonished! But there are precedents for this disguise, which has become necessary as I am leaving in a market cart.

JUNG LU. In a market cart, Old Ancestor! Where is the Phoenix Chariot?

TZU HSI. Greatness knows when to stoop. [*to Li*] Give the Emperor his peasant coat.

[*This is very rapidly done. In the meantime she addresses the crowd at the gate in her grandest manner, though she is wearing the costume of the people.*]

Now for Our tour of inspection in the frontier districts. Let us hope the local magistrates, prefects and governors will be loyally at their posts. We take this opportunity to state how much beholden We are to Her Highness, the Imperial Concubine Pearl, for the devoted manner in which she has committed suicide rather than incommode Us upon Our journey.

JUNG LU [*with an ingratiating smile*]. Yes, Her Imperial Highness has certainly shown much public spirit!

TZU HSI. Come then. Are the carts ready? Where are the Empress and the others?

EUNUCH [*at the gate*]. They are already in the carts.

TZU HSI [*as she goes out of the gate*]. I will ride in the first one and the Emperor in the second. You, Jung Lu, go back and hold the Barbarians on the southern wall as long as you can.

[*Jung Lu leaves, running. They help the Emperor up and all disappear outside the gate. Then we see, passing the gateway, the silhouette of a mule cart with the erect figure of the Empress Dowager sitting under the canopy in front of the covered compartment, and immediately following this cart a second one with the broken figure of the Emperor on the corresponding seat. Except for the cracking of the whips and the creaking of the wheels, all is silent. The last words heard come from Her Majesty the Empress Dowager, who is no longer seen.*]

Cannot Your Majesty contrive to seem a little more cheerful? Remember you are disguised as a sturdy peasant. Anyone seeing you look so miserable and bent will know at once that you are the Emperor!

[*The Emperor braces himself into some semblance of manhood and the cart passes out of sight, followed by several others.*]

END OF SCENE FOUR

[Wen Li enters, chanting a lament from the Book of Songs with ceremonial gestures and in a ritual voice]:

> 'Kio, Kio,' sings the oriole
> As it lights on the brambles.
> Who went with Duke Mu to the grave?
> That blue one, Heaven,
> Takes all our good men.
> Could we but ransom him
> A hundred would give their lives.

[Changing his voice and gestures he continues in his usual manner]:

I sang this snatch of a classical lament because we near the representation of the Holy Mother's departure to the Great Other. It is the immutable lot of all to pass there, nor was it possible for Heaven to make exception even in the case of so august a Being. As it is said in the *Analects*, 'they prayed upwards and downwards, to the spirits of Heaven above and to the spirits of the earth below.' But supplication could not avail, and to the eternal grief of Her people, She became a Guest on High.

But let me recapitulate for a moment. The inspection of rural areas which Her Majesty considered it fitting to undertake was carefully performed, much to the annoyance of the Red Barbarian Chiefs who, finding they were ignored and had lost face, begged the Mother to return to her Capital. This in due course She condescended to do. The foreign troops withdrew, and because She pitied them their long and fruitless march, She granted to them in Her infinite indulgence and bounty moneys far beyond their deserts. Thereafter, for eight years she lived content and quiet in Her Imperial City, admonishing the Emperor on his duties and watching over Her people, until the forever lamentable day, the 22nd of the 10th Moon, the thirty-fourth year of the reign of Kuang Hsu having come, She arranged what was due for arrangement, and, composing Her Valedictory Edict, departed.

As She has detailed me to oversee this drama, it is now my duty to return with my report. Though in certain passages there has been a regrettable lack of propriety, I shall find it discreet to omit reference to such lapses, and shall rather enlarge to Her upon the respectful attention with which you have watched the improving spectacle of Her life. But you will please to understand that in this prevarication I shall be actuated not by a desire to escape reprimand but by my sincere hope of making you seem to Her less barbarous than you really are. I take my leave.

[*He makes a deep bow and retires.*]

SCENE V

(The 21st of the 10th Moon, the thirty-fourth year of the reign of Kuang Hsu, November 14th, 1908.)

Her Majesty's bedchamber in the Winter Palace is a comparatively small room with a recess in which her 'kang'—a bed built of bricks and under which a fire can be made when the days are cold—is situated. The room has one peculiarity. On the walls, on every table, tea-table and desk, there is a jumble of clocks, all of different makes and sizes, some Cantonese, some European, each with a different kind of strike. Apart from these clocks, the appointments of the room follow the normal luxury of the private apartments. Besides such articles of furniture as lacquered wardrobes and chairs, embroideries, cushions and quilts, there is a dressing-table on which is every variety of scent and cosmetic, mostly of French manufacture, but not of the kind which European royalty would use. Among other pictures on the walls is a long landscape scroll of the Summer Palace and a hanging scroll of an eagle copied by Her Majesty from the original by the famous artist, the Emperor Hui Tsung of the Sung Dynasty. There is also a cabinet containing a few of Her Majesty's most cherished antiquities, such as a dragon-carp vase in red jasper, a fan painted by Shao Mi, a vase of chalcedony in the form of a citron and a lapis-lazuli table-screen inscribed with a poem of the Emperor Chien Lung's.

The Empress Dowager appears, in an everyday satin gown and without headdress, now much aged and with heavy marks under her eyes, but in no way enfeebled in spirit. She is attended by a number of ladies, maids and eunuchs, led by Li Lien-Ying.

TZU HSI. Success or failure is controlled by Heaven, and life or death is governed by Destiny. Recently I have been feeling unwell and I cannot think that my end is far distant.

1ST LADY. The Old Ancestor will live for ever!

TZU HSI. Rubbish!

2ND LADY. The Sacred Mother will live for Ten Thousand Years!

TZU HSI. Nonsense! Carry me to bed.

[*The ladies place her in bed and prop her up with pillows.*]

LI. Old Buddha will live to a hundred.

Tzu Hsi. I wish I could, Li. But I passed my 73rd birthday ten days ago and I'm now in my 74th year. I ought to be content. Yet if I could live to a hundred, then I should, I am sure, outlive the Emperor. By the way, I haven't seen him to-day.

Li. He came during Your Majesty's heart attack this morning. When I told him of this, he said he was grieved to hear it. But as soon as I assured him it would pass off, his face fell, I thought.

Tzu Hsi. Ah! His face fell! He still hopes to outlive me and take his revenge. Such natures as his feed on secret rancour. But I have never nursed vengeance. Many have I put to death, but never for that futile reason.

Li [in his privileged way]. The Holy Mother always struck first—before the other party had given cause for vengeance.

Tzu Hsi. I anticipated—yes. But tell me, Li, supposing I were to die before the Emperor—and I warn you I am already past medicine —what would happen to you?

Li. I dare not think. If I were lucky I might be allowed to commit suicide. Otherwise it would be decapitation, even perhaps dismemberment.

Tzu Hsi [with a very serious air]. It distresses me to hear you take so gloomy a view, because you are my faithful servant. Yet I cannot protect you after I am gone. Should I, then, prevent you from falling into unsympathetic hands? There are various ways of avoiding revenge. In old times faithful servitors went with their rulers to the grave, and that not only to serve again in the Other, but also to evade proscription here. Nowadays one takes a different course. I think I could help you, Li. Why risk torture and the slicing process? As I am likely to go any moment, would it not be better to make certain now?

Li [who has become more and more alarmed as she speaks]. In my grief at the thought of the Holy Mother's departure, I may have exaggerated the dangers here. If I have made enemies in discharging my duties, I have also won numerous friends. The Emperor is a merciful person . . .

Tzu Hsi. I should not trust him if I were you. I think your first view was sound. A painful death is inevitable. You will circumvent it if you are wise.

Li. I shall never forget Your Majesty's solicitude, but . . .

Tzu Hsi. No, no, I cannot let you run such a risk, Li. You see that box there? Open it.

174

[*Li, in much agitation, goes to a desk and opens the box.*]

Take out the little blue bottle.

LI [*holding up a bottle with a trembling hand*]. This one?

TZU HSI [*cheerfully*]. That is the one! Now, do you know what to do?

LI [*gasping*]. Merciful—Mother—you don't—suggest—that—

TZU HSI. Yes. Two drops are ample. It is instantaneous and painless.

LI [*his eyes starting out of his head*]. Your Majesty—orders me—to take it now?

TZU HSI [*allowing a smile at last to creep over her face*]. Ah, Li, you have not followed my meaning. Have I not told you I anticipate? Have you forgotten I always strike at the root? It is true that you would be safe by taking two drops. But there is an alternative that protects you and all my other servants just as well.

LI [*hope suddenly dawning*]. The Sacred Mother means . . .

TZU HSI. Quite so . . . in the Imperial tea preferably.

[*With huge relief and admiration, Li flings himself on the ground and kow-tows.*]

LI. The Sacred Mother is incomparably gracious to us poor souls. [*almost with gaiety in his voice*] I will now hasten to carry out the auspicious command.

TZU HSI. Go at once. I will wait for your report.

[*Li leaves, clutching the bottle.*]

Bring in the Grand Physician.

1ST LADY. Yes, Old Ancestor.

[*She goes out and conducts in a youngish, handsome man, the successor of the old Grand Physician. He kneels by the bed.*]

TZU HSI [*in her jocular way*]. I hear you have been fooling with the hearts of some of the younger ladies of my suite in the ante-chamber . . .

[*The Physician kow-tows.*]

. . . pretending that you can hear their heart troubles by means of a foreign instrument. Is it true?

PHYSICIAN [*taking a stethoscope from his sleeve*]. Yes, Your Majesty. This instrument is much used by barbarian doctors and, though averse to foreign contraptions as a rule, I have found it not unhelpful. But knowing Your Majesty's rightful contempt for the Barbarians, I dare not . . .

TZU HSI. Use it on me? I am not so old-fashioned as all that. My hair-dye comes from Paris. Come, try it.

175

[The Physician listens to her heart through the stethoscope.]
Well?
[The Physician seems to hesitate.]
I desire you to be very plain, for if my time is short, there is State business to transact.

PHYSICIAN. Your Majesty's heart is like a man stumbling under a load too heavy for him, and who may fall at any moment.

TZU HSI *[calmly]*. Just as I supposed.

PHYSICIAN. In other respects Your Majesty's constitution is quite unimpaired. Had moderation been exercised in a certain matter, Your Majesty might confidently have looked forward to ten more years of life.

TZU HSI. I know, I know. But I preferred to live fully rather than to a great age. And do not look so solemn. The many I have favoured —why, I might have included you among them! A few years ago I should have ordered you to stay.

PHYSICIAN *[very flattered]*. Your Majesty overwhelms me. Had I been so fortunate, Your Majesty would have found that the choice was a good one.

TZU HSI. Enough! I give you leave to withdraw.
[The Physician kow-tows and withdraws.]
I desire to see the Empress.
[The Empress, Lung Yu, who must have been attending in the ante-chamber, is immediately admitted. She takes her place by the bed.]

LUNG YU. Your Majesty is better? When the Grand Physician came out he seemed to be walking upon air, and looked at himself in the mirrors. There is good news?

TZU HSI *[drily]*. He was elated for another reason. *[resolutely]* No, I am not better. But first, you must know that I am expecting the sad news that the Emperor has become a Guest on High.

LUNG YU *[swallowing a sob]*. His Majesty is dead?

TZU HSI. If Heaven has seen fit to remove him, Heaven does not err.

LUNG YU *[rising]*. Have I Your Majesty's permission to withdraw? Ceremony prescribes that I superintend the rite of clothing him in the Dragon Robes of Longevity.

TZU HSI. Ceremony must wait. My time is short. Attend carefully to my words. First, send the Imperial Sedan with a strong body of Imperial Guards to Prince Chun's house at once and bring here your sister-in-law, Jung Lu's daughter, and her son, Pu Yi, your nephew and my sister's grandchild. Now, I have prepared a number of Edicts and you must announce them one by one in their correct order. The first is the Emperor's Valedictory Edict nominating the child Pu Yi for the succession of the Goodly Heritage. The second one appoints, as Regent, the young Prince Chun, the new Emperor's father. He takes orders from me who become the Grand Dowager.

LUNG YU. I trust Your Majesty will long continue to guide the State.

TZU HSI. No, I may be dead before the publication of this Edict, but do not announce my death until to-morrow. In my Valedictory Edict I command the new Regent to refer all matters of importance to you, who will take my place as Empress Dowager.

LUNG YU. I am unworthy of so high an appointment.

TZU HSI. Do not interrupt me. I have chosen you because you have been faithful to me. When the Emperor conspired, you stood by me, and later you have watched him and reported. And now, when you hear of his end, you behave with a propriety suitable to the occasion. Mark how prescient is the way of Heaven. Had he survived me, my policy would have been turned upside down. But I can place the State with confidence in your hands. You are a member of my family. Model yourself on me, and all will be well.

LUNG YU [*fervently*]. That I will try to do. But I am only a weak woman. How can I take Your Majesty's place?

TZU HSI. Have courage, as I had. I was a mere girl, far younger than you, when the Emperor Hsien Feng died and the Princes conspired to deprive me of the Regency. Many a time it was my life or the life of my enemy. Death and I have been face to face very often. But for you it will be smoother. You become Regent in your proper right. Law and precedent support you.

LUNG YU. But Your Majesty is so great that laws and precedents are created by Your Majesty's actions.

TZU HSI. I have been forced by extraordinary circumstances to act, and my actions, in turn, forged extraordinary events. When I was a girl I used to dream that either my father, my husband, my son or my nephew would be Emperor. Well, my father-in-law, my husband, my son, my nephew all were Emperors and now my grand-nephew becomes the Emperor. I ought to be content. I have been a Dowager Empress, and now am a Grand Dowager. But I was never an Empress, like you. So you are in a better position than I was, and life will be easier for you.

LUNG YU. Yet it will not be easy. The Barbarians watch for an opportunity to encroach.

TZU HSI. The Barbarians are stupid and untutored. By seeming to bend a little one can foil them. When they demanded audience, I gave it, but in the Pavilion of Purple Light, where the Tartar chieftains are received. They refused to kow-tow; I let it pass. One does not insist that a dog shall kow-tow. I even invited their women to tea and they thought me a gentle, kind old lady. How I laughed! Gentle and kind! Had I been that, I'd have been dead long ago.

[*Spirited though her talk is, the Empress Dowager has visibly weakened. The Empress, the Ladies-in-Waiting and the eunuchs kneel by the bedside. Some are weeping. But Tzu Hsi seems to be holding on, waiting for something.*]

Do not grieve. I am happy. My life has been very full. My conscience is clear. Those I have condemned were a danger to the State or they foolishly sought to get the better of me. And why let oneself be worsted by fools? But I have never forgotten a friend, however humble. Once a Magistrate lent me three hundred taels. I was poor and the money saved me. I did not forget. He became a viceroy.

[*Her voice becomes fainter and she looks round her again. At this moment Li appears by a side door, crosses the stage, replaces the bottle and kneels by the bed. By a scarcely perceptible sign he intimates to his mistress that he has carried out her commands. Then, in a toneless voice, he announces the death of the Emperor.*]

LI. His Majesty, the Emperor Kuang Hsu, has started his grand journey to become a Guest on High.

[*As the Empress and other ladies begin to sob as ceremony prescribes, Tzu Hsi smiles, and all look at her in silence.*]

TZU HSI. All is well. And now bring me the Phoenix Robes of Longevity, and play some music. Play 'Moonset on the Bridge of Dreams'.

[*They play softly while her ladies wrap her in the robes.*]

Now that my days are over, there is one thing I regret: I have never had leisure to master the classics, nor to practise as I wished calligraphy, painting and music. Turn me now to the Quarter of Happy Augury—the South.

[*They move her gently to face the South.*]

A mirror [*which they immediately place in her hands*] and some flowers [*which are also given to her*]. Please dress my hair.

[*They dress her hair and decorate it with flowers.*]

慈
禧
太
后

EMPRESS DOWAGER TZU HSI

(. . . a gentle, kind old lady)

My Ancestors have come to meet me!

[*There is a long silence and they become aware that she is dead. Presently Li rises to his feet and facing the audience formally announces the event giving all her titles in a rhythmical chant.*]

LI. The Motherly and Auspicious; the Orthodox and Blissful; Prosperous, All-Nourishing; Radiant, Sedate; the Dignified, Perfect; Long-Lived, the Dutiful; Reverend, the Praiseworthy; Worshipful, Illustrious; the Grand Empress-Dowager has mounted the Phoenix and ridden away to Western Heaven.

END OF SCENE FIVE

END OF ACT THREE